the human machine

« AN OWNER'S GUIDE TO THE BODY »

WELCOME PAGE

We share our planet with an incredible range of life – millions of species of animals, plants, fungi and micro-organisms. Although we are the most intelligent of all life forms, we are, like other creatures, biological machines that walk, feed, drink and behave. And, in our case, talk, create, think and remember.

The Human Machine is a unique guide to the human body and the way it works. It is a user's manual that covers every aspect of body activities, including troubleshooting and repairs. On each and every page of this book you can discover everything you need to know and understand about the body's huge range of operations.

Like any manual, *The Human Machine* is highly organized. Check out any aspect of the body machine's workings and you will be presented with the categories you can see opposite. What better way, as an owner, to discover more about your body and how it works.

Richard Walker

Richard Walker PhD

HOW TO USE THIS BOOK

RIVAL PRODUCTS

Take a look beyond the human species to see how animal and plants perform and compare with us.

? TRUE OR FALSE

Tricky, testing statements will make you question whether they are real facts or mere inventions.

DESIGN FEATURES

At a glance, this enables you to pick out the key features of every aspect of the human machine.

ADDITIONAL DATA

Here's an extra snippet of information that adds to the main theme and gives you more insight into the body's workings.

SPOT CHECK

A chance to test your knowledge with multiple choice questions. The answers are found at the foot of the right-hand page.

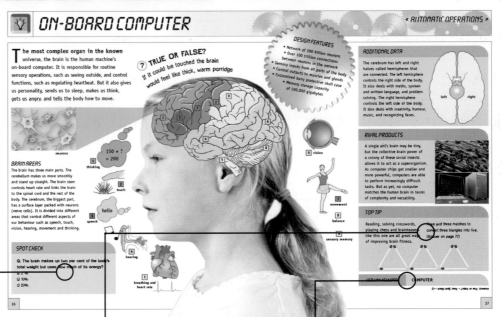

TOP TIP

See how to make the most of your life in terms of health, diet, exercise and general well-being.

WEBLINK KEYWORD

Turn to pages 72–73 for a full, indexed list of websites that will add to your understanding of the human machine.

SYSTEM CHECK

Teamwork makes the human machine operate efficiently. The 'team' consists of twelve specialised body systems that interact and work together to produce a walking, talking human being. Let's check on some of those systems.

FUELLING

Your mouth is the entrance to the digestive system. This long, tubular system gets food into the body, then breaks it down into very simple substances. The body uses these to provide the energy it needs to work, along with the raw materials required to repair it and make it grow.

CONTROL

You can see and understand the words and pictures in this book because of your nervous system. It also enables you to feel the pages, smell lunch, remember what happened yesterday, invent stories, and throw a ball without falling over. In fact, the nervous system controls just about everything we do. And like other body machine systems it is made up of component parts called organs – in this case, the brain, spinal cord and nerves.

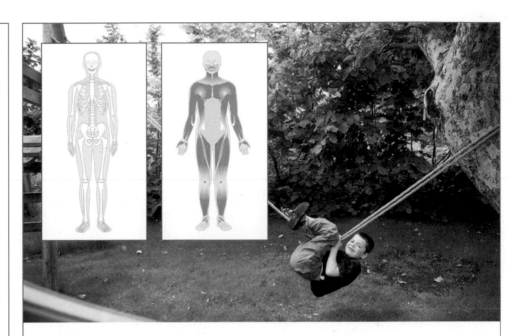

MOVEMENT

Two systems keep you upright, give the human machine its shape and allow you to move. These are the skeletal and muscular systems. The skeleton is a flexible scaffolding made of bones which is pulled by muscles so you can perform a vast array of movements from writing to climbing a rope.

DELIVERY

Without vital supplies, the body machine wouldn't last long. The breathing system gets oxygen into the body. The circulatory (blood) system carries oxygen, food and other essentials to every single part of the body.

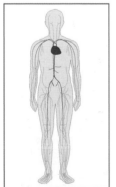
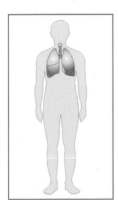

Each of us has our own individual appearance and personality, but we also share key features. Our bodies, built from trillions of cells using the same masterplan, grow and age in identical ways.

PRODUCT SPECIFICATION

Every body machine is constructed to the same pattern with minor variations in certain features such as height, weight, shape, eye colour and personality. These differences distinguish us one from another and make each of us unique. But otherwise we are all the same – brainy animals with upright bodies supported by two legs, and with hands free to reach out and grasp.

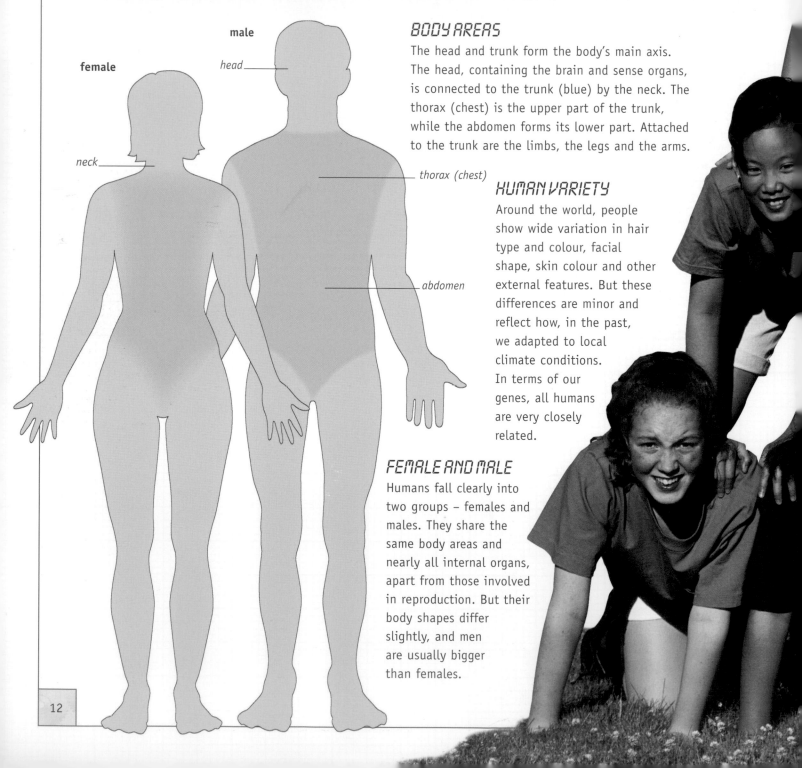

female

male

head

neck

thorax (chest)

abdomen

BODY AREAS

The head and trunk form the body's main axis. The head, containing the brain and sense organs, is connected to the trunk (blue) by the neck. The thorax (chest) is the upper part of the trunk, while the abdomen forms its lower part. Attached to the trunk are the limbs, the legs and the arms.

HUMAN VARIETY

Around the world, people show wide variation in hair type and colour, facial shape, skin colour and other external features. But these differences are minor and reflect how, in the past, we adapted to local climate conditions. In terms of our genes, all humans are very closely related.

FEMALE AND MALE

Humans fall clearly into two groups – females and males. They share the same body areas and nearly all internal organs, apart from those involved in reproduction. But their body shapes differ slightly, and men are usually bigger than females.

12

DESIGN FEATURES

- Ability to walk on two legs
- Hands free to perform tasks
- Opposable thumb enables hand to grip objects and make tools
- Short body hair means humans can sweat to keep cool
- Flexible arms and shoulders
- Large brain size means greater intelligence

? TRUE OR FALSE?

We have just as many hairs as chimpanzees – just shorter

RIVAL PRODUCTS

Humans belong to a group of mammals (animals with fur that feed their young on milk) called primates. They include, apart from us, the orang-utan (top right), gorilla (centre right) and chimpanzee (bottom), our closest relative. Many millions of years ago we and the other apes shared a common ancestor. Today, while we big-brained humans thrive, our relatives are endangered.

SPOT CHECK

Q. How many humans are there on Earth?

a) Around 6 billion
b) Around 60 million
c) Around 6 million

WEB LINK KEYWORD	SPECIFICATION

Answers: True or False? – True; Spot Check – a)

PRODUCT LIFE SPAN

Every living thing on Earth has an expected life span – the period of weeks, months or years it is expected to remain alive. But how long can the human machine be expected to keep on working and how can we make it run for longer? Crucial factors include genes (inherited instructions) and the machine's lifestyle.

RECORD BREAKERS

Wherever we look in the animal and plant worlds there are examples of individuals living to the extremes of their normal life span. At 122, Frenchwoman Jeanne Calment (1875-1997) has the longest confirmed human life span. That's nothing compared with Adwaita, a giant tortoise that died aged 250 in 2006. But this Californian bristlecone pine was already 300 years old when the Egyptian pyramids were being built 4,700 years ago.

RIVAL PRODUCTS

For most animals, the bigger they are, the longer they live. But that's not the only factor. If it was, humans would have the same life span as pigs (10 years). Another key factor is the ratio between brain and body sizes. With big brains and smallish bodies we live far longer than predicted by body size alone.

Mouse	Rabbit	Dog	Penguin	Kangaroo	Gorilla
3 years	*9 years*	*12 years*	*15 years*	*18 years*	*35 years*

(?) TRUE OR FALSE?

One day humans may
be able to live to 150

LIFE PROFILE

During its life, the body machine
goes through a set sequence of physical
changes. During childhood, the body
grows rapidly. Adolescence involves a
growth spurt, and the child changes
into an adult. In adulthood, growth is
completed. In later life, the skin
wrinkles, hair greys, and the machine
becomes less efficient until it stops
working altogether.

DESIGN FEATURES
- Parental care for offspring from 0-18 years
- Brain designed for rapid learning in first 15 years
- Capable of reproduction from 12-14 years onwards
- Built-in replacement schedule

TOP TIP

TO LIVE TO 100:

Avoid too much sun

Avoid stress

Eat well

Take regular exercise

ADDITIONAL DATA

Birds have life spans that
are much longer than would
be predicted by their body
or brain sizes. So, if you
want to live longer, sprout
wings and learn to fly!

SPOT CHECK

**Q. Which country has the
longest life expectancy?**
a) USA   b) Russia   c) Japan

WEB LINK KEYWORD	LIFE SPAN

Answers: Spot Check – c) then b); True or False? – Maybe

Macaw	Dolphin	Elephant	Human
50 years	65 years	75 years	80 years

15

The basic components of the body machine are microscopic living structures called cells. There are over 200 different types of cell in the body. Cells of the same type are organized into communities called tissues while different types of tissues work together to form organs such as the heart and brain. This organization converts a shapeless mound of cells into a living human being.

CELL STRUCTURE

Cells may be small but they're not simple. Each is a self-contained living unit with an outer membrane, a controlling nucleus, and, between the two, a jelly-like cytoplasm. Within the cytoplasm are various tiny organelles, each with their own task. Mitochondria supply energy to make things work, while ER and the Golgi body make, store and transport materials.

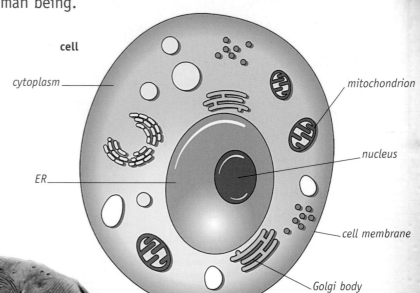

cell

cytoplasm

mitochondrion

nucleus

ER

cell membrane

Golgi body

This needle tip and dust mite have been magnified over 400 times

● a cell would appear this size

? TRUE OR FALSE? All living things are made from cells

CELL SIZE

Before the invention of the microscope no one realized that something as small as a cell could exist. To get an idea of the size of a 'typical' cell you can see it here compared to a mite on the the point of a needle. The body's biggest cell, the egg or ovum, is about three times bigger than this, just visible to the naked eye.

DESIGN FEATURES

- Self-reproducing
- Built-in energy supply
- 24/7 service for replacing worn-out cells
- Cell membrane controls imports and exports
- Nucleus contains cell assembly instructions
- Built-in manufacturing, storage and distribution network
- Available in a wide range of models

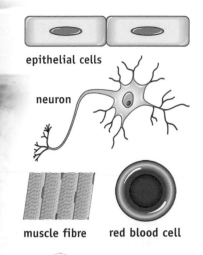

epithelial cells

neuron

muscle fibre   red blood cell

bone cell   fat cell

VARIETY

The size and appearance of each type of cell is related to the job it performs. For example, tightly-packed epithelial cells line the mouth and other openings. Long, spiky neurons pick up and relay nerve messages. Cylindrical muscle fibres contract to move the body. Doughnut-shaped red blood cells carry oxygen. Bone cells maintain our bones. And spherical fat cells store fat.

RIVAL PRODUCTS

Cells use atoms, joined together as molecules, to make their mitochondria, membranes and other working parts. The new science of nanotechnology does exactly the same. Each coloured sphere in this nano-machine represents an atom. By transmitting power through two shafts this microscopic machine works like the gears in a car.

SPOT CHECK

Q: How many cells are needed to build a body machine?
a) 100 billion (100,000,000,000)   b) 100 million (100,000,000)
c) 100 trillion (100,000,000,000,000)

WEB LINK KEYWORD	**CELLS**

Answers: *True or False?* – True; *Spot Check* – c)

17

EXTERNAL FEATURES

Separating the human machine's delicate inner workings from the harsh outside world is the skin. This external covering is made of two layers. The outermost, the tough epidermis, is constantly worn away and replaced. The lower, thicker layer, the dermis, contains blood vessels and sensors. Available in a range of colours, skin also provides add-ons including hairs and nails.

IN THE SWIM

Without skin, we'd lack the protective coat that stops water getting inside the body, watering down the blood, and disrupting cells. There would be no melanin, the brown colouring that filters out the harmful UV radiation in sunlight. And there would be nothing to stop germs invading deep into every part of the body.

epidermis

hair

germ

skin helps to stop germs getting inside the body

TEST YOUR PRODUCT
PINCH TEST

Skin becomes less elastic as we age. Grip a fold of skin on the back of your hand, pull it upwards, then release it. It should quickly flatten. Do the same to someone older. Their skin should take longer to flatten.

? TRUE OR FALSE?
Fingernails grow faster in summer than winter

18

exposure to sunlight
can harm the skin

ADDITIONAL DATA

What would we do without nails?
These clear, hard coverings that
protect the tips of fingers and
toes grow from the epidermis,
the upper layer of the skin.
Fingernails help us to grip objects
and pick them up, or to play the
guitar. And they're invaluable for
scratching annoying itches.

RIVAL PRODUCTS

Insects, including this darkling
beetle, belong to a massive group
of animals called arthropods. They
have a hard outer covering called
an exoskeleton. Reptiles have a
tough, scaly skin and some, such
as this chameleon, can change
their skin colour to indicate their
mood or as camouflage.

SPOT CHECK

Q: How much does an adult's skin weigh?

a) 500g

b) 2kg

c) 5kg

DESIGN FEATURES

- Self-repairing
- Waterproof and germproof
- Filters harmful UV rays in sunlight
- Helps control body temperature
- Full range of touch, heat, cold, and pain sensors
- Produces hairs and nails
- Built-in oil release system keeps surface supple

WEB LINK KEYWORD	SKIN

Answers: True or False? – True; Spot Check – c)

19

REPLACEMENT MODELS

As the years pass, the body machine inevitably wears out and eventually stops working. Fortunately, humans are equipped with a reproductive system that can produce children to replace people who age and die. The male reproductive system releases cells called sperm that fertilize (fuse with) a female egg to make a fertilized egg. This divides repeatedly to produce a fetus which grows inside its mother's uterus (womb) and develops into a baby.

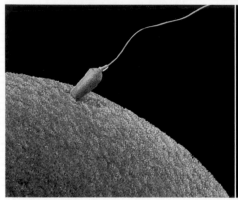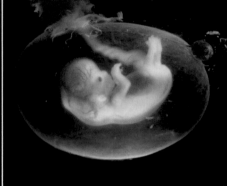

FERTILIZATION

A male sperm pushes its way into a female egg cell at fertilization. The sperm nucleus fuses with the egg nucleus to produce a library of instructions that will be used to build a new human being.

8/10 WEEKS

The developing baby, now called a fetus, is the size of a strawberry and begins to look human. You can see its head, trunk, arms and legs. Inside its body all the heart and other organs are in place.

20 WEEEKS

Eyelids, lips, fingers and toes are now in place. The umbilical cord (far right) is the lifeline supplying food and oxygen that links fetus to mother.

RIVAL PRODUCTS

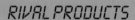

Many plants, such as this dandelion, reproduce by producing seeds, which are dispersed away from their parents. The seeds contain embryo plants packaged with a food store so they can grow into new plants. Many animals, such as green turtles, reproduce by laying eggs that hatch to release smaller versions of their parents.

BIRTH

Once the fetus is fully developed it is ready to leave its mother's uterus and begin its life in the outside world. The uterus contracts to push the baby out of the mother's body. Once this process is complete the newborn, exposed to a new world of sound and light, takes her first breaths, and the umbilical cord is cut.

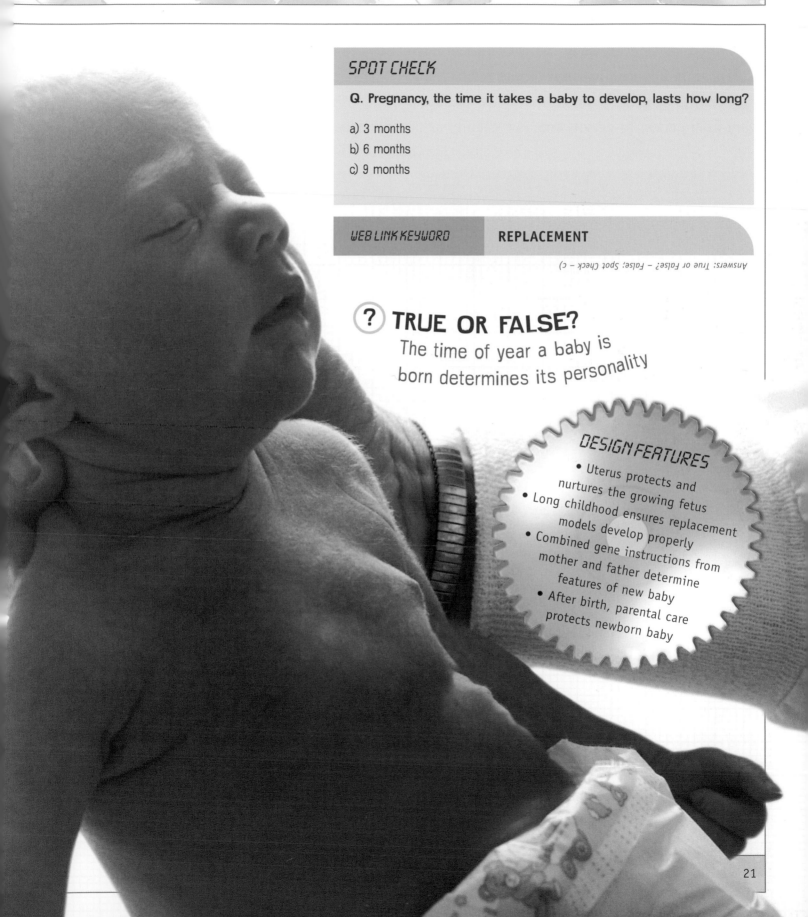

SPOT CHECK

Q. Pregnancy, the time it takes a baby to develop, lasts how long?

a) 3 months
b) 6 months
c) 9 months

WEB LINK KEYWORD	REPLACEMENT

Answers: True or False? – False; Spot Check – c)

? TRUE OR FALSE?

The time of year a baby is born determines its personality

DESIGN FEATURES

- Uterus protects and nurtures the growing fetus
- Long childhood ensures replacement models develop properly
- Combined gene instructions from mother and father determine features of new baby
- After birth, parental care protects newborn baby

MACHINE INSTRUCTIONS

Stored inside every body cell is the set of instructions to build and operate a human machine. These instructions are called genes. All of us have the same genes – which is why we all appear human. But some genes vary from person to person and give each of us our individual features.

INHERITED FEATURES

From each parent, we inherit a genome, or one set of genes. As a result, you have some of your mother's features and some of your father's. There may be some features that have skipped a generation – your grandparents may have them, but your parents don't. Inherited features, which may run in the family, include ginger hair, 'hitchhiker's' thumb, and the ability – or not – to tongue roll.

DNA

DNA base

DNA INSTRUCTIONS

Genes are carried in chromosomes, tightly-coiled strands made from the chemical DNA. Inside most of your body's cells are 46 chromosomes – 23 inherited from your mother and 23 from your father. DNA resembles a twisted ladder, its 'rungs' or bases forming the 'words' of the instructions.

(?) TRUE OR FALSE?

We share 85 per cent

of our genes

with mice

TEST YOUR PRODUCT
FAMILY TREE

Compare photos of
yourself with those of
your parents and, if you
have any, your brothers
and sisters, as well as
your grandparents. Can
you see any features
that have been 'passed
on' from one generation
to the next?

grandparents

parents

child

ADDITIONAL DATA

Because we have two sets of genes, there may be one version
of a particular gene in one set, and a different one in the
other. For example, take the gene for eye colour. If you have
one 'blue' gene and one 'brown' gene, your eyes will probably
be brown because the 'brown' gene is dominant.

RIVAL PRODUCTS

None – all living things contain DNA

SPOT CHECK

How many genes are there in a single genome?

a) 250   b) 2,500   c) 25,000

WEB LINK KEYWORD	INSTRUCTIONS

DESIGN FEATURES

- Two sets of genes inside most cells
- Two metres of DNA packed inside each cell nucleus
- Genes inherited from both parents
- Genes determine appearance of body machine
- Genes are digital instructions encoded in DNA

Answers: True or False? – True; Spot Check – c)

BIOMECHANICS

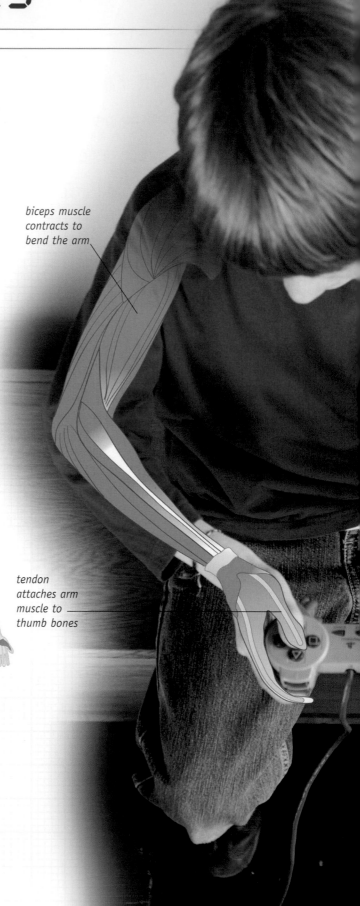

biceps muscle contracts to bend the arm

Without its framework of bones the human machine would collapse in a shapeless heap. Bones create a strong but flexible supporting framework called the skeleton. This is covered by layers of skeletal muscles, so called because they pull bones to make the body run, jump and perform many other movements. Muscles also shape the human machine and maintain posture by holding the body upright.

MAKING MOVEMENT

How is this boy able to use this game console? The answer lies in biomechanics, the study of how movement happens. His hands are very flexible because each is made from 27 bones, many with flexible joints between them. Muscles – most extending from his forearm but some in his hand – cross the joints between bones they are attached to and contract (shorten) to make the bones move. These muscles work in a precise order under the control of the brain.

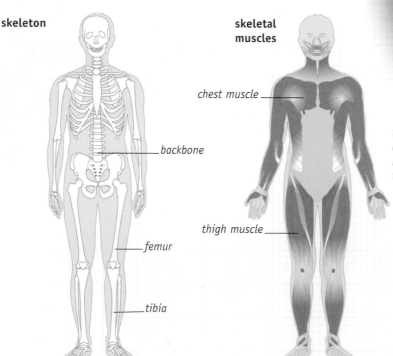

skeleton

skeletal muscles

chest muscle

backbone

tendon attaches arm muscle to thumb bones

femur

thigh muscle

tibia

(?) TRUE OR FALSE?
Muscles can push bones but not pull them

24

DESIGN FEATURES

- 206-bone skeletal framework
- Bones weight-for-weight six times stronger than steel
- Pulling power of 650 skeletal muscles
- Joints between bones give skeleton flexibility
- Bone self-repair facility
- Flexible, shock-absorbing backbone

TEST YOUR PRODUCT
MUSCLE FATIGUE

Make a fist with your fingers. Now open it. Repeat this action as quickly and as many times as you can. Your hand will soon get tired. That's because the muscles that move your body are strong but fatigue (tire) easily.

upper arm bone

forearm bone

wrist bone

RIVAL PRODUCTS

Humans are neither the fastest movers on the planet, nor the slowest. While a snail glides slimily at 0.05 km/h an athlete can sprint at up to 36 km/h, and a cheetah, the quickest land animal, reaches 100 km/h. But the peregrine falcon, the fastest of all animals, can dive at up to 320 km/h.

ADDITIONAL DATA

Bones may appear dry and dead but they are not. Day by day, small changes – removing a bit of bone here and adding some there – reshape bones. If you exercise regularly, your bones are reshaped to make them as strong as possible.

SPOT CHECK

Q. Which is the longest bone in your body?

a) Humerus (upper arm bone)

b) Femur (thighbone)

c) Tibia (shinbone)

WEB LINK KEYWORD

BIOMECHANICS

Answers: True or False? – False; Spot Check – b)

WIRING AND COMMUNICATION

Operating the body machine would be impossible without built-in wiring and communications in the form of the nervous system. It is made from billions of interconnected nerve cells, called neurons, that carry electrical signals, called impulses, at lightning speed. The nervous system allows us to feel, to think and to move.

(?) TRUE OR FALSE? Nerve cells can last a whole lifetime without being replaced

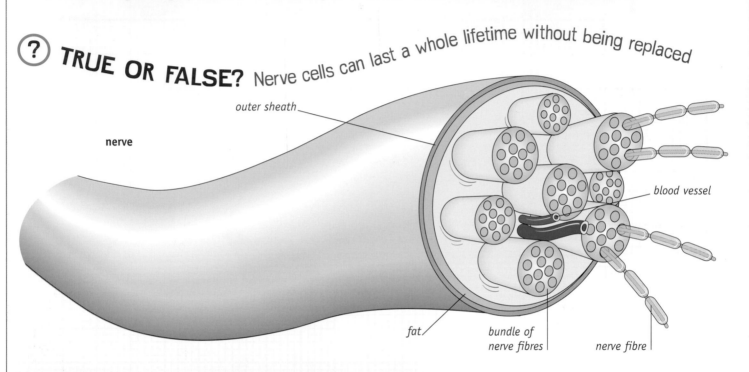

outer sheath

nerve

blood vessel

fat

bundle of nerve fibres

nerve fibre

RIVAL PRODUCTS

The Internet is a vast global network of interconnected computers that allows many millions of users to share, receive and send out information. However, despite the power of this technology, it is still no match for the faster and smarter human brain and nervous system.

NERVE BUNDLES

Nerves are the 'cables' that emerge from the brain and spinal cord to relay nerve messages around the body. Each nerve is made up of bundles of nerve fibres, the long impulse-carrying extensions of neurons. The bundles are bound together, along with blood vessels and protective fat, by a protective, bendy sheath.

nerve

brain

spinal cord

THE NERVOUS SYSTEM

Controlling and co-ordinating almost all the body machine's activities is the nervous system. At its core is the central nervous system (CNS) – the brain and spinal cord. Inside the CNS billions of neurons receive information from all parts of the body, process it, and send out instructions. Information is relayed between CNS and all body parts, from toes to teeth, by nerves.

DESIGN FEATURES

- Central information processing unit – the brain
- Multi-tasking features – sensing, thinking, moving
- Automatic control of body activities
- Spinal cord relay system between brain and body
- High-speed message transfer

TEST YOUR PRODUCT
REACTION TIMES

You'll need a ruler and a friend. Hold the ruler at the very tip between finger and thumb. Your friend must catch the ruler when you drop it. Note the place on the ruler where it's caught. Swap over. Is your measurement smaller – and reaction time faster?

SPOT CHECK

Q. At what speed do the fastest nerve impulses travel?

a) 350 km/h   b) 35 km/h   c) 3.5 km/h

WEB LINK KEYWORD	WIRING

Answers: ; True or False? –True ;Spot Check – a)

INTERNAL TRANSPORT

T he trillions of cells that make up the body machine need to be nurtured constantly to avoid system malfunctions. Non-stop care and attention is provided by the body's internal transport network, the circulatory system. Blood, pumped by the heart along tubes called blood vessels, carries oxygen, food, warmth and other essentials to cells and removes their wastes for disposal.

CIRCULATORY SYSTEM

Blood is pumped around the body through two loops. The heart has two sides, each with an upper atrium and lower ventricle. Oxygen-depleted blood (blue) from the body enters the right atrium, and is pumped by the right ventricle to the lungs to pick up oxygen before returning to the left atrium. The left ventricle pumps oxygen-rich blood (red) to the body's oxygen-hungry cells. Arteries carry blood away from the heart, veins towards the heart. Tiny vessels called capillaries link arteries and veins.

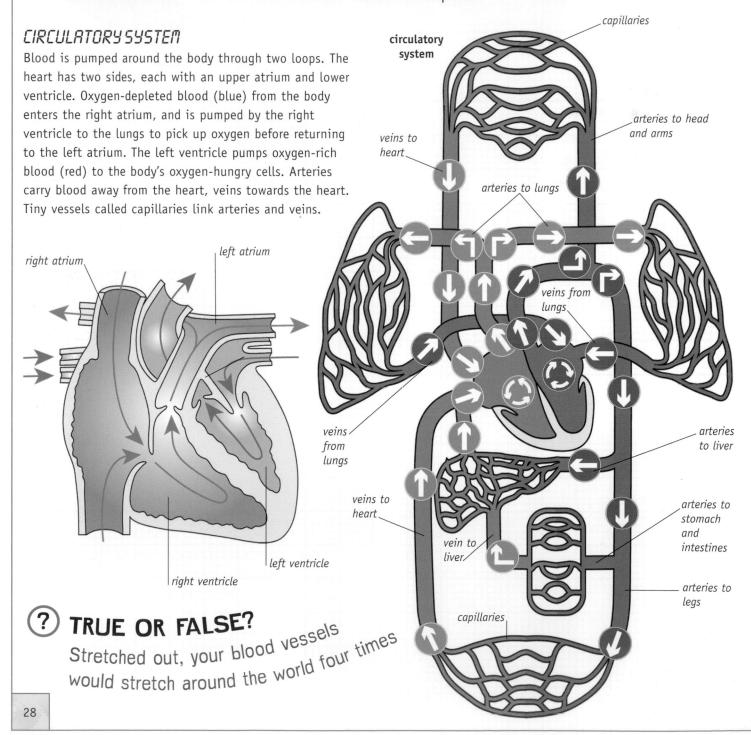

right atrium

left atrium

left ventricle

right ventricle

circulatory system

capillaries

arteries to head and arms

veins to heart

arteries to lungs

veins from lungs

veins from lungs

arteries to liver

veins to heart

vein to liver

arteries to stomach and intestines

arteries to legs

capillaries

(?) TRUE OR FALSE?

Stretched out, your blood vessels would stretch around the world four times

DESIGN FEATURES

- Blood vessel network reaches all parts of the body
- Every cell has dedicated delivery service provided by capillaries
- Blood delivers essentials to cells and removes wastes
- Heart works constantly without tiring

TEST YOUR PRODUCT
MEASURING HEART RATE

Do this by feeling your pulse, the surge of blood along an artery every time your heart beats. Put two fingers on your wrist and count the number of pulses for a minute. That is your heart rate. Do the same after exercise. Your heart rate increases to get extra oxygen to your muscles.

BLOOD

About five litres of this red liquid flow through blood vessels. Blood consists of oxygen-carrying red blood cells, which give blood its colour, and a yellow fluid called plasma in which float white blood cells. These defend the body against disease. Plasma carries food and chemical messengers called hormones along with waste produced by body cells. Blood also distributes heat around the body.

RIVAL PRODUCTS

This lightweight pump (below right) can be attached to a severely damaged heart to help it work properly. Artificial blood (below left) has been developed by scientists for people who have lost blood; it can be used with any blood group and is disease-free.

TOP TIP

Good health depends on keeping the circulatory system working at its best. This means regular exercise, and a varied diet without too much fat or salt.

SPOT CHECK

When we are resting, our hearts beat on average:

a) 25 times per minute
b) 75 times per minute
c) 125 times per minute

WEB LINK KEYWORD	**CIRCULATION**

AUTOMATIC OPERATIONS

Controlling how much light enters our eyes is just one of many of the human machine's automatic functions. These enable the body to run itself, giving us the freedom to sense, to think and to communicate.

VENTILATION

Oxygen, one of the gases in the air around us, is key to the body's operations. Our cells use it to release the energy stored in glucose, which we get from food, and this drives body processes. Releasing energy also produces a poisonous waste called carbon dioxide. Breathing, or ventilation, gets oxygen into the body and gets rid of carbon dioxide.

BREATHING AIR

The business of breathing revolves around the two spongy lungs that fill most of the space in your chest. Air travels to the lungs through the nose – where it is warmed and cleaned – throat, and trachea (windpipe) which branches into left and right bronchi. Movements of the ribs and diaphragm – a sheet of muscle underneath the lungs – breathes air into, and out of, the lungs.

(?) TRUE OR FALSE?

There are over 300 million alveoli in your two lungs

trachea (windpipe)

right lung

left lung

bronchus

RIVAL PRODUCTS

Not all animals use lungs to breathe. Earthworms take in oxygen from the air through their moist surface. Insects, such as this praying mantis, breathe through small holes that pipe air around the body. Fish get oxygen from the water they swim in through their gills.

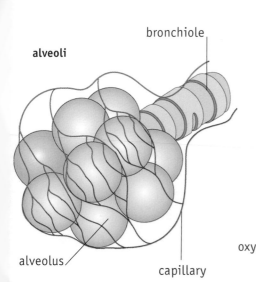

alveoli

bronchiole

alveolus

capillary
network

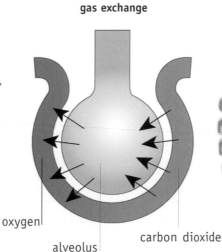

gas exchange

oxygen

alveolus

carbon dioxide

DESIGN FEATURES

- Built-in nasal air filter
- Automatic ventilation mechanism
- Tennis court-sized surface for taking in oxygen packed inside chest
- Automatic adjustment of breathing rate during exercise
- Flexible ducting links lungs to nose
- 24/7 expulsion of waste carbon dioxide

EXCHANGING GASES

The lung's bronchi branch into smaller and smaller branches, eventually becoming tiny bronchioles no wider than a hair that end in bunches of rounded air bags. Enclosed by blood capillaries, these alveoli provide a massive surface for exchanging gases. Oxygen from breathed-in air passes from the alveolus into the bloodstream to be carried away to cells. Carbon dioxide moves in the opposite direction to be breathed out.

ADDITIONAL DATA

Smoking cigarettes damages the lungs and the rest of the breathing system. Cigarette smoke contains chemicals that can cause cancer. Smoking makes people unfit and short of breath. Over time it also makes skin more wrinkly.

TEST YOUR PRODUCT
CATCH YOUR BREATH

Breathe onto a mirror, or a pane of glass, to see what happens. It should mist up because the air you breathe out has been warmed and moistened while inside your lungs. On the cool glass surface, water vapour in the breathed-out air condenses to produce a fine mist.

SPOT CHECK

Q. What percentage of the air is made up by oxygen?

a) 1%

b) 21%

c) 91%

WEB LINK KEYWORD   **VENTILATION**

Answers: True or False? – True; Spot check – b)

REFUELLING

Eating food every day is essential to refuel the human machine and keep it working. The nutrients in food supply energy to power the body's activities as well as the raw materials needed for growth and repair. But these nutrients are 'locked' inside big molecules. These have to be broken down into smaller nutrient molecules that can be used by our cells.

BREAKING DOWN

In many factories, products are made by fitting together different components. In the human machine, digestion – breaking down food into its basic parts – works in the opposite direction. Mechanical digestion – being crushed by the teeth or churned by the muscular wall of the stomach – turns solid food into a thick soup. Chemical digesters called enzymes also get to work. They split big molecules into smaller ones that can be absorbed into the bloodstream.

DESIGN FEATURES

- Automatic swallowing
- Built-in chop and crush feature
- Hunger feature automatically signals need for refuelling
- Range of enzymes to digest different foods
- Automatic release of digestive juices at mealtimes
- Long intestines for efficient digestion and absorption
- Regular emptying of waste

TEST YOUR PRODUCT
STARCH TO SUGAR

You'll need a piece of white bread. Put it in your mouth and chew it for two minutes. Notice how the taste changes. It should taste bland at first, then sweet. That's because an enzyme in saliva (spit) digests bland-tasting starch in bread into sweet-tasting sugars.

Here is the digestive system, pulled from the body and stretched out. From food being eaten to waste being expelled takes between 24 and 48 hours.

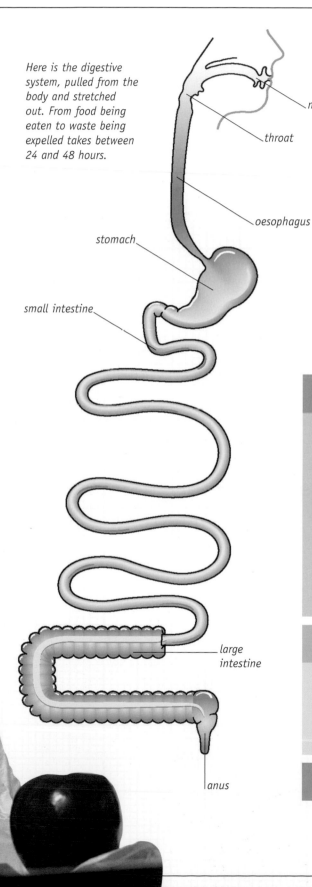

mouth

throat

oesophagus

stomach

small intestine

large intestine

anus

(?) TRUE OR FALSE?
An average person eats 30 tonnes of food in a lifetime

DIGESTIVE SYSTEM

This consists of a tube – some nine metres long – that extends from mouth to anus. After the food is chewed in the mouth and swallowed, it is pushed down the oesophagus to the stomach. Here it is pummelled into a soup and part digested. In the small intestine, enzymes complete digestion and nutrients are absorbed into the bloodstream and carried to hungry body cells. Any undigested food passes along the large intestine and is expelled through the anus.

RIVAL PRODUCTS

Living things display a range of refuelling techniques. Fungi, such as bread mould, release enzymes, then absorb the liquid remains. Trees and other plants use sunlight to convert water and carbon dioxide into sugars. Some animals, such as this mosquito (right), feed on the blood of other animals.

SPOT CHECK

Q. How many teeth do adults have in their upper and lower jaws?

a) 16 + 16   b) 10 + 10   c) 14 + 18

WEB LINK KEYWORD   FUEL

ON-BOARD COMPUTER

The most complex organ in the known universe, the brain is the human machine's on-board computer. It is responsible for routine sensory operations, such as seeing outside, and control functions, such as regulating heartbeat. But it also gives us personality, sends us to sleep, makes us think, gets us angry, and tells the body how to move.

neurons

BRAIN AREAS

The brain has three main parts. The cerebellum makes us move smoothly and stand up straight. The brain stem controls heart rate and links the brain to the spinal cord and the rest of the body. The cerebrum, the biggest part, has a surface layer packed with neurons (nerve cells). It is divided into different areas that control different aspects of our behaviour such as speech, touch, vision, hearing, movement and thinking.

SPOT CHECK

Q. The brain makes up two per cent of the body's total weight but uses how much of its energy?

a) 2 %

b) 10%

c) 20%

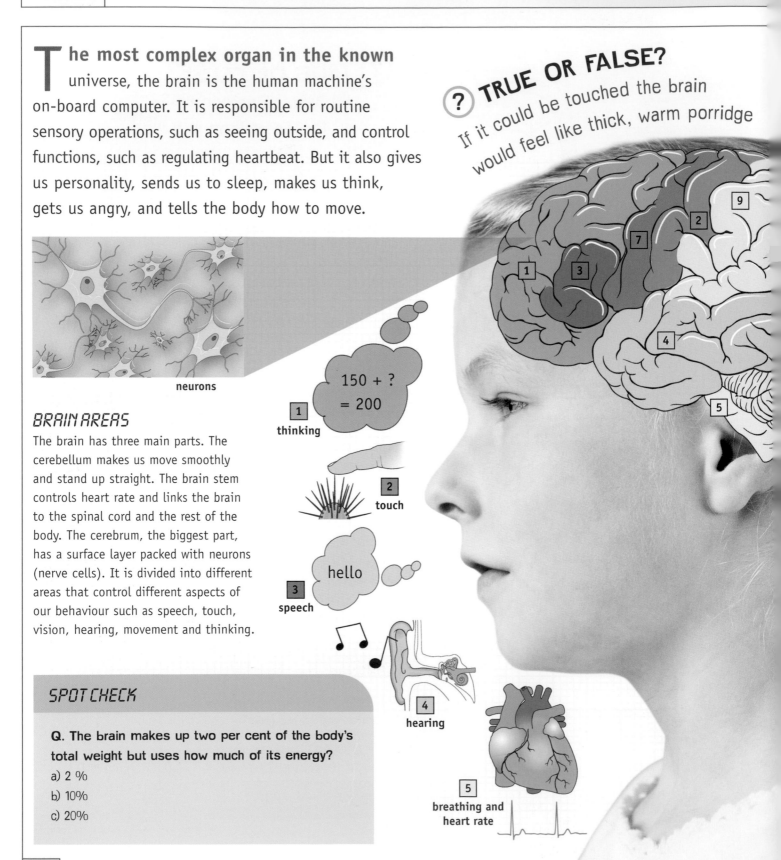

? TRUE OR FALSE?
If it could be touched the brain would feel like thick, warm porridge

150 + ? = 200

1 thinking

2 touch

hello

3 speech

4 hearing

5 breathing and heart rate

36

DESIGN FEATURES

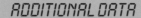

- Network of 100 billion neurons
- Over 100 trillion connections between neurons in the network
- Sensory inputs from all parts of the body
- Control outputs to muscles and glands
- Customized bony protective skull case
- Memory storage capacity of 100,000 gigabytes

6

8

6 **vision**

7
movement

8
balance

9
sensory memory

ADDITIONAL DATA

The cerebrum has left and right halves called hemispheres that are connected. The left hemisphere controls the right side of the body. It also deals with maths, spoken and written language, and problem solving. The right hemisphere controls the left side of the body. It also deals with creativity, humour, music, and recognizing faces.

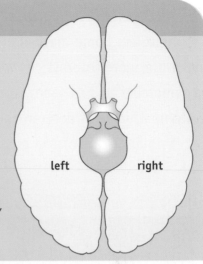

left   right

RIVAL PRODUCTS

A single ant's brain may be tiny, but the collective brain power of a colony of these social insects allows it to act as a superorganism. As computer chips get smaller and more powerful, computers are able to perform increasingly difficult tasks. But as yet, no computer matches the human brain in terms of complexity and versatility.

TOP TIP

Reading, solving crosswords, playing chess and brainteasers like this one are all great ways of improving brain fitness.

Move just three matches to convert three triangles into five. (Answer on page 73)

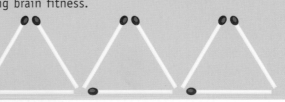

WEB LINK KEYWORD   **COMPUTER**

Answers: True or False? – True; Spot Check – c)

The brain is equipped with special built-in features. Some make life less hazardous, others make life more interesting, while others enable us to remember and to learn. In charge is the limbic system, which lies deep in the cerebrum, the 'thinking' part of the brain.

SADNESS HAPPINESS

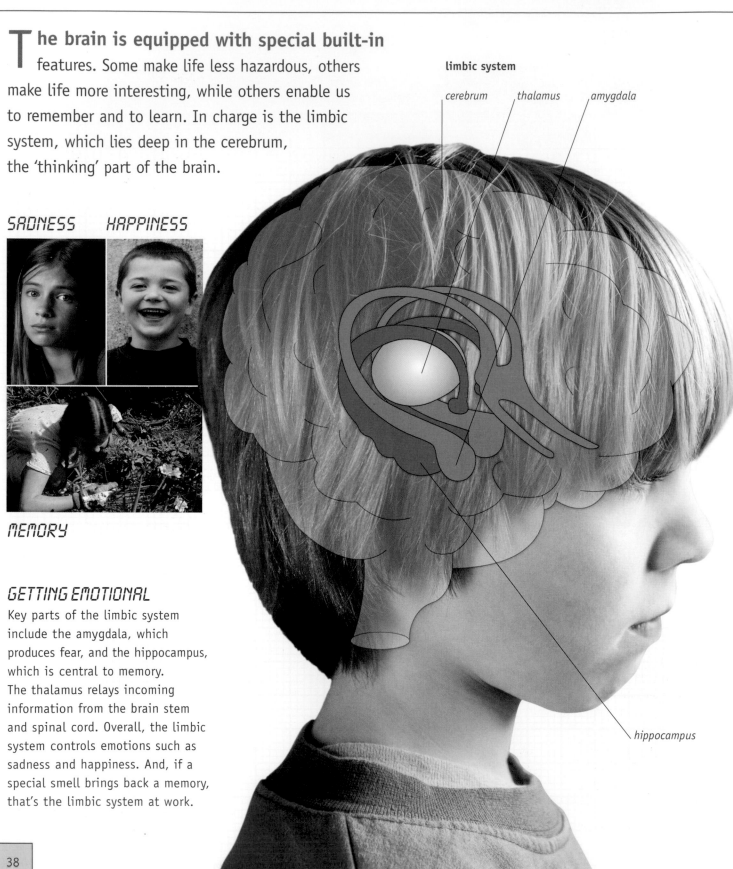

MEMORY

GETTING EMOTIONAL

Key parts of the limbic system include the amygdala, which produces fear, and the hippocampus, which is central to memory. The thalamus relays incoming information from the brain stem and spinal cord. Overall, the limbic system controls emotions such as sadness and happiness. And, if a special smell brings back a memory, that's the limbic system at work.

limbic system

cerebrum   thalamus   amygdala

hippocampus

DESIGN FEATURES

- Limbic system controls built-in emotions
- Fear function protects human machine against threats
- Emotions make life more interesting
- Massive memory storage facility
- Learning module active throughout life

REMEMBER AND LEARN

Facts, faces, events, skills... The human brain has an incredible facility to remember things. We retain some memories for just a short time and then discard them. More important ones are shuttled repeatedly between the hippocampus and cerebrum until they are filed in long-term memory. Long-term memory plays a crucial role in learning, from a child's first steps to understanding a foreign language.

TEST YOUR PRODUCT
MEMORY TEST

Ask a friend to collect 20 different objects. Take two minutes to look at the objects and memorize them. Then ask them, in your absence, to hide five of the objects. On your return, can you name all five? Repeat the test and see if you can improve your memory.

? TRUE OR FALSE?

Fear of phobias is called phobophobia

RIVAL PRODUCTS

A frightened cat automatically stands tall to make itself look bigger and more threatening as part of a pre-programmed response to enemies. In the African savanna, wildebeest have an in-built system that makes them migrate at the same time each year to find new feeding grounds and sources of water.

ADDITIONAL DATA

Fear is important because it can alert us to dangerous situations. Some people, however, develop phobias to certain objects and situations. A phobia is an irrational fear of something that is usually harmless, such as this spider.

SPOT CHECK

Q. Which of these words describes an irrational fear of spiders?

a) Ailurophobia

b) Arachnophobia

c) Apiphobia

WEB LINK KEYWORD	MEMORY

Answers: *True or False? – True; Spot Check – b) (a) is cats, c) is bees]*

39

SHUTDOWN MODE

We know that sleep is vitally important to all of us because without it we feel tired and ill. Each evening a natural mechanism built into the brain gradually reduces its activity so we go from being wide awake to feeling sleepy. Each morning the reverse happens and we wake up. During sleep the body has a chance to rest, while the brain has time to sort and process the previous day's experiences.

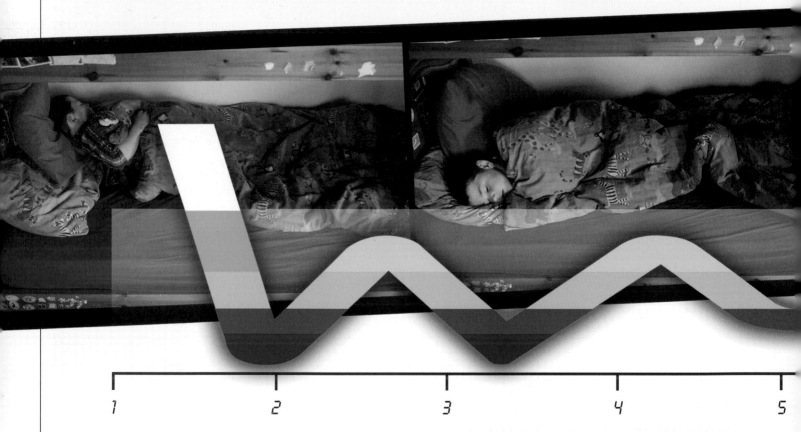

1   2   3   4   5

SLEEP PATTERNS

Each night, two types of sleep follow each other repeatedly, as shown by this graph. We doze off and slip through stages of NREM (non-rapid eye movement) sleep into deep sleep. This is followed by lighter REM (rapid eye movement) sleep, when the body, apart from the eyes, cannot move.

DREAMS

Many scientists think dreams are produced when the brain 'replays' daily experiences so that they get shunted into permanent, long-term memory. Dreams are played out mainly during REM sleep.

RIVAL PRODUCTS

Koalas snooze for 20 hours a day to save energy. Migrating birds, such as swifts, take lots of short naps in the air. Dolphins sleep with only one half the brain 'switched off' to make sure they don't drown.

40

DESIGN FEATURES

- Automatic night-time shutdown facility triggers sleep
- Automatic decrease in breathing, heart rate and body temperature
- Emergency wake-up mode when 'things go bump in the night'
- Endless variety of dreams available
- Optional snoring feature
- Automatic daytime wake-up mechanism ends sleep

⊘ TRUE OR FALSE?

In all, people spend around one-third of their lives asleep

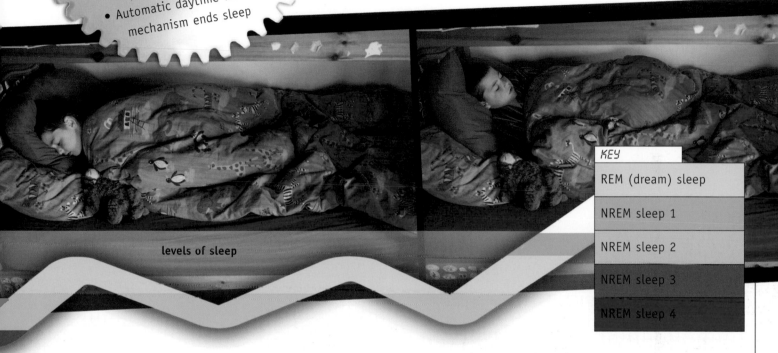

levels of sleep

KEY

REM (dream) sleep

NREM sleep 1

NREM sleep 2

NREM sleep 3

NREM sleep 4

timeline hours

6   7   8   9

ADDITIONAL DATA

This sleeping man's head is 'wired up' to an EEG machine. This detects and displays 'brainwaves', the patterns of electrical activity produced by his brain cells. Brainwave activity is much 'busier' during REM sleep than deep sleep.

SPOT CHECK

Q. How many hours sleep does the average young adult need?

a) Seven hours
b) Nine hours
c) Five hours

| WEB LINK KEYWORD | **SLEEP** |

Answers: True or False? – True; Spot Check – b)

ENVIRONMENTAL SENSORS

I n order to operate, **the body machine** has to sense and react to changes in its surroundings or environment. The smell of smoke, for example, can alert it to danger, while the taste of ice cream can provide enjoyment. A battery of sensors detect stimuli – changes – and send messages to the brain which interprets and responds to them.

DESIGN FEATURES
- Millions of smell sensors in the nasal cavity inside the nose
- Versatile skin sensors that detect touch, pressure, vibration, heat, cold, and pain
- Hands and lips most sensitive parts of skin
- Ten thousand taste buds in the tongue
- Ears detect pitch, loudness and direction of sound

? TRUE OR FALSE?
The human nose can distinguish over 10,000 different smells

RIVAL PRODUCTS

Some animals can sense things we cannot. Rattlesnakes can 'see' the heat given off by prey at night with sensors that detect infrared radiation. Honeybees can detect patterns in flower petals that are invisible to us because they can 'see' ultraviolet light. And bats use ultrasound, too high-pitched for us to hear, to navigate and catch insect prey.

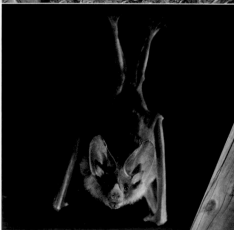

THE SENSES

Sensors give us our senses – taste, touch, hearing and smell. The fifth, vision, is so important that it has its own pages (46-47). Taste buds in the tongue detect sweet, sour, salt, bitter and umami (meaty) tastes. Millions of skin sensors allow us to feel objects. Sensors deep inside the ear detect sounds. And smell sensors high up in the nose enable us to smell flowers, enjoy food and avoid danger.

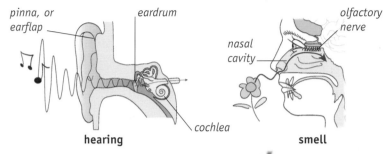

pinna, or earflap

eardrum

olfactory nerve

nasal cavity

cochlea

hearing

smell

taste

sweet taste area

nerve

touch

TEST YOUR PRODUCT
TASTE TEST

You will need a friend, a blindfold, a nose clip, and several different types of food, such as pretzels, chocolate and apple, cut into small pieces. Blindfolded and with a nose clip, how many food items can your friend identify by taste alone? Probably not many.

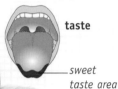

SPOT CHECK

Q. The loudness of sounds is measured in
a) Decapods
b) Megabytes
c) Decibels

Answers: True or False? – True; Spot Check – c)

WEB LINK KEYWORD   **SENSORS**

43

Of all the body's senses, vision is the most important. It allows the human machine to interact with and navigate around its surroundings. The sense organs that make vision possible are the two eyes, housed in protective sockets in the front of the skull. They contain millions of light detecting sensors that send messages to the brain.

SEEING IN ACTION

Light reflected from an outside object passes through the cornea, the clear part of the eye, and through the pupil. The cornea focuses the light, as does the clear lens, to produce a sharp, upside-down image of the skateboarder on the retina. This layer of light sensors covering the inside of the eye sends messages along the optic nerve to the back of the brain. Here, in the visual area, those signals are turned into pictures that you can 'see'.

left eyeball

optic nerve

visual area of brain

brain

retina

⑦ TRUE OR FALSE?
If you sneeze with your eyes open, your eyeballs will pop out

TEST YOUR PRODUCT
FIND YOUR DOMINANT EYE

Discover whether your left or right eye is dominant. Choose an object 2m away. Stare at the object and point at it using an index finger – you will see two blurry fingers. Close each eye in turn. When your dominant eye is open, your finger will point directly at the object.

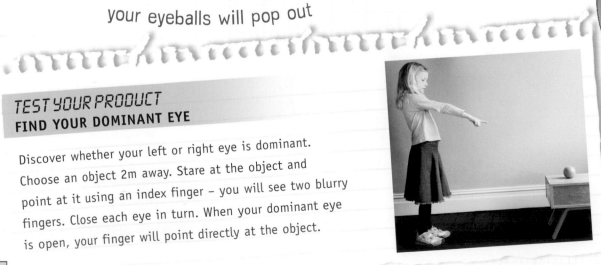

DESIGN FEATURES

- Blink and wipe-clean function
- Automatic light-level control
- Multidirectional in-socket movement
- Automatic focusing
- Analogue-digital conversion
- Full colour operation on most models
- High-speed link to brain via optic nerve

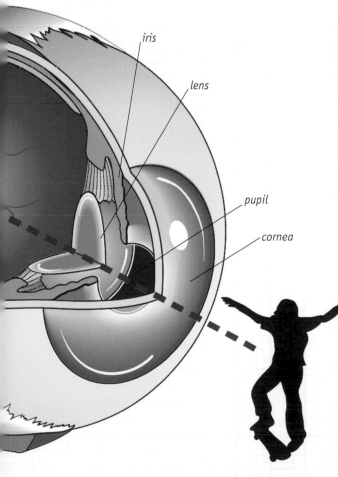

iris

lens

pupil

cornea

ADDITIONAL DATA

How much light enters the eye is controlled automatically by the iris, the coloured part of the eye. In dim light, the iris makes the pupil wider (top). More light enters the eye so you can see more clearly. In bright light, it makes the pupil – the black hole at its centre – narrower (bottom) so you are not dazzled.

RIVAL PRODUCTS

With its single lens, the eye of the squid (top), and other top molluscs, like the octopus, is surprisingly similar to the human eye. The insect eye (bottom) – called a compound eye – is made of many units each with its own lens. It has an amazing ability to detect rapid movement.

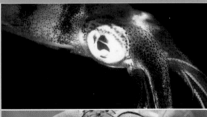
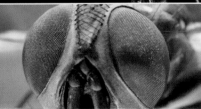

SPOT CHECK

Q. Over what distance can the human eye detect a lighted candle at night?
a) 100 metres away   b) 1,000 metres (1 km) away
c) 10,000 metres (10 km) away

| WEB LINK KEYWORD | **VISION** |

Answers: True or False? – False; Spot Check – b)

OPTICAL TESTS

Throughout the day, your brain has to make sense of the constant stream of signals it receives from your eyes. It uses a wide range of visual clues to work out the identity, shape, size, colour and other features of the scene before you. But the human machine isn't foolproof. The brain can be tricked into seeing things that aren't the same way in reality. You can test this out with the optical illusions on these pages.

SEEING THINGS

Sometimes the brain adds things that aren't there. The white triangle (below) doesn't really exist. Your brain created it using remembered information. The grey 'dots' that appear in the grid (right) are produced when sensors in the eye send confused signals to the brain.

DIFFERENT SIZES?

The brain calculates the size of an object with the help of clues in the background. If those clues are confusing, the brain can be easily misled. Here, the sloping lines create the illusion that the girl on the right is bigger than the one on the left. Check them with a ruler – they are all the same size.

(?) TRUE OR FALSE? Both eyes 'see' exactly the same view of the outside world

COLOUR CONFUSION

Look at the two groups of red squares. At first glance, the top group appears to be a different shade to the bottom group. In fact, they're identical. The different coloured bars, however, fool the brain into thinking that the squares are not the same shade.

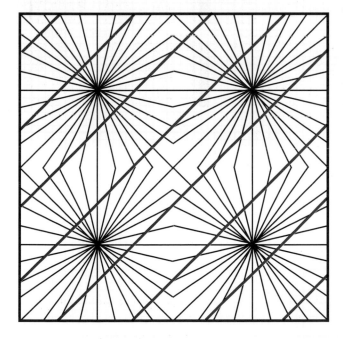

DESIGN FEATURES
- Brain fills gaps when there is insufficient information from eyes
- Faces only recognized by brain if seen the right way up
- Brain judges object's shape according to its background
- Brain judges object's size according to its background
- Brain judges an object's colour by its surroundings

STRAIGHT OR CURVED

Believe it or not, every line in this image is a straight line. The background pattern of black lines distorts the diagonal red lines so that they appear curved. To check this, take a ruler and hold its edge against one of the red lines.

SPOT CHECK

Q. Which part of your brain analyses signals from the eyes so you can see?
a) Front b) Top c) Back

WEB LINK KEYWORD   **TESTS**

Answers: True or False? – False; Spot Check – c)

COMMUNICATION SYSTEMS

We humans are social beings who enjoy and need company. Communication plays a key role in the way we live because, for example, it enables us to make friends and show how we feel. The ways by which we communicate include body language and facial expressions. But by far the most powerful communication tool is unique to humans – speech enables us to pass on ideas, thoughts and intentions to one or many people.

SENDING MESSAGES

You can tell how someone feels by facial expressions (left) such as smiling and frowning. These are produced by over 30 small muscles that pull on the skin of the face. Body language (top right), such as these aggressive/defensive postures, clearly reveal a person's intentions and thoughts. New methods of communication (top left) include e-mail and websites.

? TRUE OR FALSE? It takes more muscles to frown than to smile

RIVAL PRODUCTS

Animals use a wide range of communication techniques. Male fiddler crabs have one claw much larger than the other to attract mates and deter rival males. Monkeys and apes use grooming to bond with each other.

DESIGN FEATURES

- Voice modules include speech and singing
- 'Organ pipe' amplification of sounds by throat and nose
- Available languages include Chinese, English, Spanish and hundreds of others.
- Language enables information to be transmitted between generations
- Widest range of facial expression in the animal kingdom

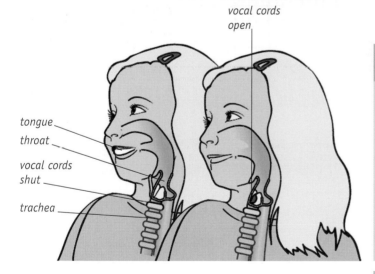

vocal cords open

tongue
throat
vocal cords shut
trachea

ADDITIONAL DATA

Sign language is used by many people who find hearing difficult. Finger, hand, arm, and body movements, along with facial expressions and lip patterns, are used as a substitute for speech.

SPEECH

The larynx sits on the trachea, the tube that leads to the lungs. Stretched across the larynx are two vocal cords. During normal breathing these are wide open. When we speak they are stretched shut. Controlled bursts of air from the lungs make the stretched vocal cords vibrate and produce sounds. These sounds are turned into understandable speech by the tongue, teeth and lips.

SPOT CHECK

Q. Which side of the brain controls speech?

a) Both sides   b) Left   c) Right

WEB LINK KEYWORD	COMMUNICATION

Answers: True or False? – False; Spot Check – b)

HEATING AND COOLING

R egardless of whether the outside world is boiling hot or freezing cold the temperature inside the body machine must be kept constant. Why? Because otherwise its trillions of cells refuse to work at their best. Body heat is generated mainly by the busy liver and moving muscles, spread by the blood, and then lost through the skin.

TOO HOT

RIVAL PRODUCTS

The body temperature of reptiles, such as this lizard, changes with the outside temperature. On cool mornings, lizards bask in the sun to warm themselves so they become active. In hot, tropical countries, termites build tall nests with built-in 'air-conditioning' to keep the insect colony cool during the day and warm during the chilly night.

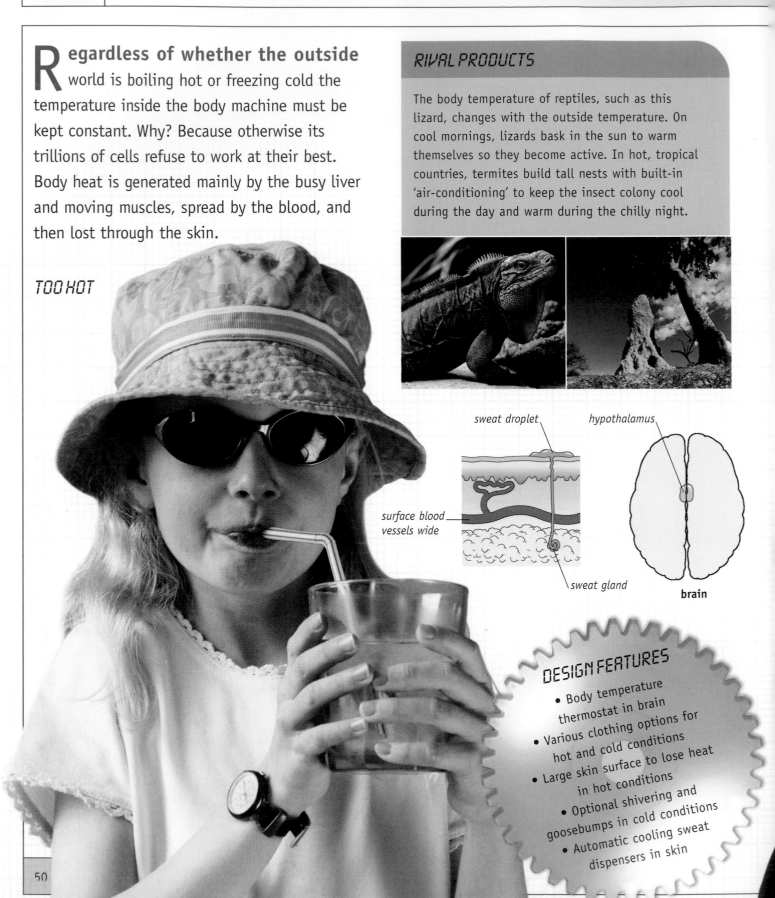

sweat droplet

hypothalamus

surface blood vessels wide

sweat gland

brain

DESIGN FEATURES
- Body temperature thermostat in brain
- Various clothing options for hot and cold conditions
- Large skin surface to lose heat in hot conditions
- Optional shivering and goosebumps in cold conditions
- Automatic cooling sweat dispensers in skin

STAYING THE SAME

To cope with changing outside temperatures, the brain's hypothalamus controls heat loss through the skin. When it's very hot, blood vessels in the skin get wider and lose extra heat from the warm blood they are carrying. The skin's sweat glands release sweat which evaporates from the skin's surface to cool the body down. When it's cold, blood vessels get narrower so less heat is lost.

TOO COLD

TEST YOUR PRODUCT
SWEAT TEST

Put your hand inside a clear plastic bag. Use an elastic band to loosely hold the bag around your wrist. Look at the bag over the next 30 minutes. You should be able to see tiny water droplets that have evaporated from sweat on your skin.

(?) TRUE OR FALSE?
You lose over 30 per cent of body heat through your head

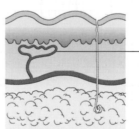

surface blood vessels narrow

SPOT CHECK

Q. What is normal body temperature for humans?
a) 47°C
b) 37°C
c) 27°C

WEB LINK KEYWORD	HEAT

Answers: True or False? – True; Spot Check – b)

51

CHEMICAL CONTROL

The nervous system isn't the sole body controller. The endocrine system consists of several glands that release chemical messengers called hormones into the bloodstream. Each hormone changes the activity of specific targets. Feedback mechanisms, which work a bit like a room thermostat, maintain the right levels of each hormone in the blood.

(?) TRUE OR FALSE?

Hormones take much longer to work than the nervous system

EMPTY

FULL

MASTER GLAND

Hanging from the base of the brain, the small pituitary gland is vitally important. Overseen by the brain's hypothalamus, the pituitary releases hormones that control growth, urine volume, and birth. It also triggers other endocrine glands to release hormones to control reproduction and metabolism.

GLUCOSE LEVELS

It's vital to keep constant levels of glucose fuel in the blood regardless of whether the human machine is empty (between meals) or full (after a meal). Two hormones, called insulin and glucagon, ensure that cells are neither deprived of, nor swamped with, glucose.

DESIGN FEATURES
- Efficient transport of hormones in bloodstream
- Network of endocrine glands in head, neck and trunk
- Feedback system automatically regulates hormone levels
- Designated target tissues
- Long-term effects

HORMONES IN ACTION

Hormones control a very wide range of activities. Adrenal gland hormones help us manage stress (right), while other hormones from the pituitary gland control the production and release of a mother's breast milk after a baby is born (far right). Sex hormones released by the ovaries and testes trigger puberty (below) and control reproduction.

RIVAL PRODUCTS

Female moths release special chemicals called pheromones into the air that males detect using their antennae. In early summer, rising hormone levels change the colour of the male stickleback's belly from silver to blue and red to encourage a female to lay her eggs.

SPOT CHECK

Q. Which of these is not a hormone?

a) Somatotropin

b) Adrenalin

c) Haemoglobin

WEB LINK KEYWORD   **SURVIVE**

Answers: True or False? – True; Spot Check = c)

WASTE AND WATER

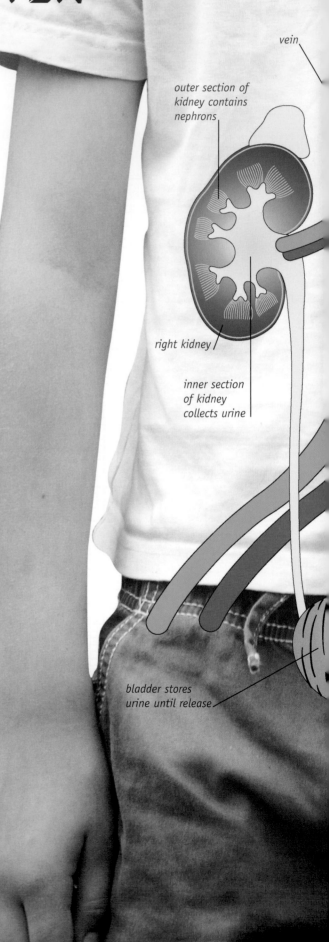

vein

outer section of
kidney contains
nephrons

right kidney

inner section
of kidney
collects urine

bladder stores
urine until release

The kidneys filter unwanted wastes made by cells from the blood, along with excess water. Inside the kidneys millions of microscopic tubes called nephrons filter fluid from the blood. Most of the water and dissolved substances are returned to the bloodstream, leaving waste and water, which are released from the body as urine.

BLOOD FILTER

Every day 1,800 litres of blood flow through the kidneys. Fluid that could fill almost 200 one-litre bottles is filtered from blood into the nephrons. But just 1.5 litres of waste and water passes out as urine.

HOT SWEAT

Some water and a little waste is also lost from the body as sweat, especially on hot days, or during exercise. The more water that is lost by sweating, the lower the volume of urine produced by the kidneys.

ADDITIONAL DATA

Water is essential for life, which is why keeping constant levels of water inside the body is so important. Water content varies with age and sex. For example infants are 73% water, young men 60%, young women 50%, and older persons 45%.

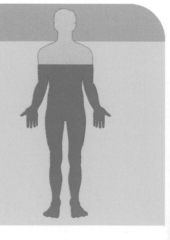

artery

left kidney

ureter carries
urine to bladder

urethra carries
urine to the
outside

DESIGN FEATURES
- Built-in sensor in brain warns of low water levels in body by producing sensation of thirst
- Kidneys filter blood and produce urine every second of the day
- Urine released several times a day when convenient
- Warning system tells brain when bladder is full

⑦ TRUE OR FALSE?
Doctors can diagnose diseases by measuring levels of substances in urine

RIVAL PRODUCTS

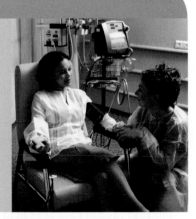

If the kidneys stop working properly, a dialysis machine, or artificial kidney, can be used to remove waste products and excess water from the blood. The process usually takes up to six hours and is performed several times a week.

SPOT CHECK

Q. Which is the main waste substance in urine?

a) Uric acid
b) Carbon dioxide
c) Urea

WEB LINK KEYWORD   **WASTE**

Answers: True or False? – True; Spot Check – c)

SURVIVAL MODE

The body machine first appeared in the warm, comfortable climate of Africa. Over many thousands of years humans have spread to most parts of the Earth and have learned to deal with extremes of cold, heat and altitude. Survival strategies include wearing clothes to keep warm, building shelters and homes, and exploiting new sources of food.

COLD NORTH

The Inuit peoples of Greenland, northern Canada, Alaska and Siberia are experts in surviving in some of the coldest, harshest conditions on Earth. The fish, seals, whales, musk oxen and other polar animals that they hunt traditionally provide food, heat, light, tools and shelter. Animal furs are made into clothes that keep out the cold. Their short, broad stature also means that they lose heat more slowly than tall, thin people.

? TRUE OR FALSE?

On mountain tops there is more oxygen in the air than at sea level

ADDITIONAL DATA

Below 27°C the naked body machine is no longer able to keep its body temperature at a steady 37°C without stoking up its internal 'furnace' to release more heat. Wearing clothes and heating our homes helps us to stay at the optimum body temperature.

DESIGN FEATURES

- Built-in heat generation facility
- Insulating fat layer under the skin
- Inventive brain develops modern technology to aid survival
- Intelligent brain enables body machine to develop strategies to adapt to extremes of climate.
- Heat loss system (sweating) to survive hot conditions

LOW OXYGEN

In conditions of low or no oxygen, the human machine cannot operate. But technology allows us to get round this problem. In space, where there is no oxygen, an air supply and pressurised suit keep astronauts alive. Under water, where the small amount of oxygen can't be breathed, a scuba diver carries an air supply.

RIVAL PRODUCTS

To survive cold winters, the dormouse surrounds itself with leaves and grasses and goes into a state of body shutdown called hibernation. In Antarctica, the coldest place on Earth, Emperor penguins huddle together to keep warm and survive the winter months.

SPOT CHECK

Q. Where is the hottest place on Earth?

a) Death Valley, California

b) Dallol Depression, Ethiopia

c) El Alizia, Libya

WEB LINK KEYWORD **SURVIVE**

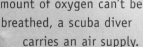

Answers: True or False? – False; Spot Check – c)

MAINTENANCE AND UPGRADES

Like any machine, the body's workings can be upset by outside interference or inner wear and tear. Internal maintenance mechanisms work to minimize damage, while upgrades may improve the way we work.

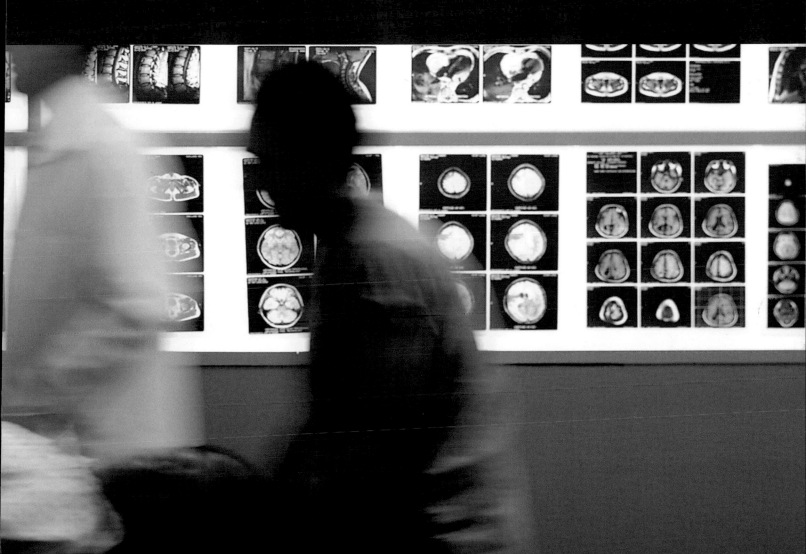

BUILT-IN PROTECTION

Normally the body machine operates without problems. But sometimes one or more parts go wrong, and we get ill. Many problems, or diseases, are caused by tiny micro-organisms called pathogens or germs, including bacteria, viruses and protists. They threaten the body 24/7, and once inside can multiply and cause disease. Fortunately, the body's defences – the immune system – usually stop that happening.

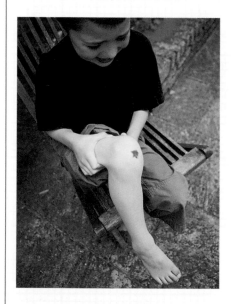

Wound healing

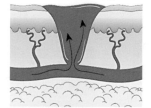

1. Cut in skin

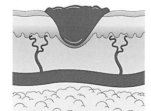

2. Clot

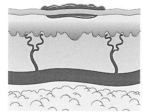

3. Scab

DEFENCES IN ACTION

If the skin, the first line of defence, gets cut (1), blood leaks out and germs get in. Blood thickens and forms a clot (2) that dries into a scab (3) which covers the repair zone. Invading pathogens are hunted and eaten by marauding white blood cells such as macrophages (right). If there are any escapees, chemicals called antibodies are released. These disable specific pathogens, and remember their identity should they ever invade again.

(?) TRUE OR FALSE?

There are over 100 different viruses that can cause the common cold

OVER-REACTING

Allergies happen when the body machine's defences over-react to something that poses no threat to it, making its owner ill. People can become sensitive to a whole range of items – called allergens – including pet hair, pollen, or foods such as peanuts.

————— macrophage

————— bacteria

DESIGN FEATURES

- Multi-level defences
- First level defences include skin, tears, saliva
- Built-in blood clotting and scab formation facility
- Tears and saliva contain bacteria-killing chemicals

ADDITIONAL DATA

Bacteria are not the only pathogens. The flu virus (right) is one of several tiny chemical packages that cause disease in humans. Protists are one-celled organisms, some of which are pathogens, including Giardia (below, right) which causes really bad diarrhoea.

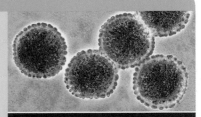

SPOT CHECK

Q. Which of these diseases is not caused by a pathogen?

a) Measles
b) Malnutrition
c) Mumps

WEB LINK KEYWORD   **PROTECT**

Answers: True or False? – True; Spot Check – b)

EMERGENCY MODE

Dangers or threats to the human machine can sometimes happen so quickly that there is no time to even think about the action you should take to avoid injury. Fortunately, the body has an emergency mode that launches automatic, high-speed reactions called reflexes that deal with danger before you are even aware of it.

TEST YOUR PRODUCT
STARTLE REFLEX

Surprise your friend. Clap your hands suddenly and loudly just in front of their face but take special care not to hit them. Their eyelids close automatically. This is an example of a reflex, in this case, one that protects the eyes from possible harm.

READY FOR ACTION

When faced with a threat, the body primes itself for action. Nerve signals from the brain, reinforced by the hormone adrenalin, cause heart and breathing rates to increase, blood glucose levels to rise, and extra blood to be diverted to muscles. These changes power up the body to run away from the threat or to confront it.

RIVAL PRODUCTS

Lizards have a neat way of getting out of trouble. If their tail is grabbed by a predator it drops off, allowing the lizard to make its escape. Some animals, such as this inflated puffer fish, make themselves as big as possible to scare away enemies.

ADDITIONAL DATA

If you touch something sharp or hot, you pull away your hand automatically. This automatic action is called a withdrawal reflex. Nerve signals from your hand go to your spinal cord and straight back to arm muscles that pull your hand away.

DESIGN FEATURES

- Built-in body protection mechanisms
- High speed nerve signals cause instantaneous reactions
- Adrenalin back-up option available in serious situations
- Automatic reflex responses to threats

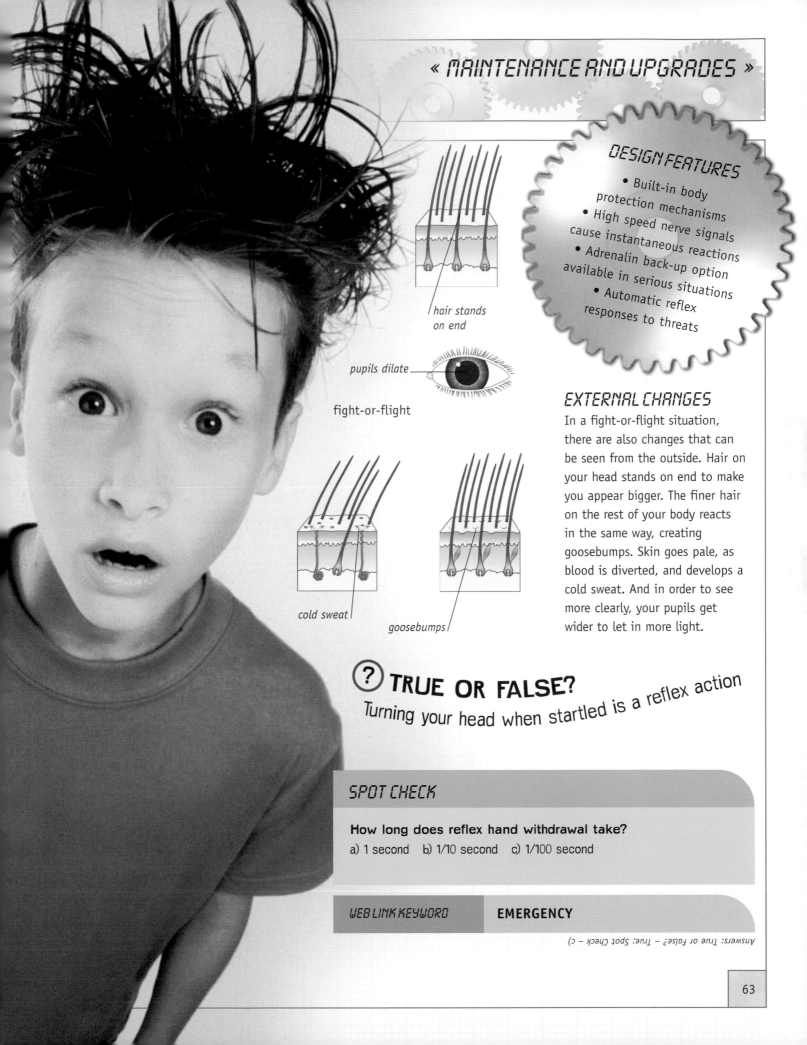

hair stands on end

pupils dilate

fight-or-flight

cold sweat

goosebumps

EXTERNAL CHANGES

In a fight-or-flight situation, there are also changes that can be seen from the outside. Hair on your head stands on end to make you appear bigger. The finer hair on the rest of your body reacts in the same way, creating goosebumps. Skin goes pale, as blood is diverted, and develops a cold sweat. And in order to see more clearly, your pupils get wider to let in more light.

⑦ TRUE OR FALSE?

Turning your head when startled is a reflex action

SPOT CHECK

How long does reflex hand withdrawal take?
a) 1 second   b) 1/10 second   c) 1/100 second

WEB LINK KEYWORD   **EMERGENCY**

Answers: True or False? – True; Spot Check – c)

TECHNICAL SUPPORT

They may be sophisticated and efficient, but sometimes the body's defence and repair systems need a helping hand. Accidents and disease-causing organisms, or pathogens, can threaten the body's normal workings. Fortunately, modern medicine can provide technical support in the form of diagnosis, surgery, drugs, vaccines and other solutions to get the human machine back on track.

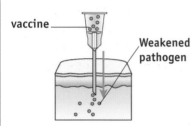

vaccine

Weakened pathogen

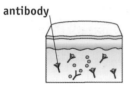

antibody

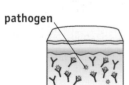

pathogen

SURGERY

Surgery, the repair or replacement of diseased or damaged body tissues, takes place in the operating theatre. Doctors and nurses wear gowns, masks and gloves, and use sterile instruments, to avoid infecting the patient.

VACCINATION

Vaccination prepares the body to fight off pathogens which can infect the body very quickly. Weakened pathogens are injected through the skin and force the defence system to make pathogen-disabling antibodies. When the 'real' pathogen invades, masses of antibodies are released and infection is halted.

RIVAL PRODUCTS

Some people treat disease with 'alternative' medicine. Reflexology, for example, uses foot massage to 'benefit' other parts of the body. Inserting sterile needles during acupuncture 'balances energy'.

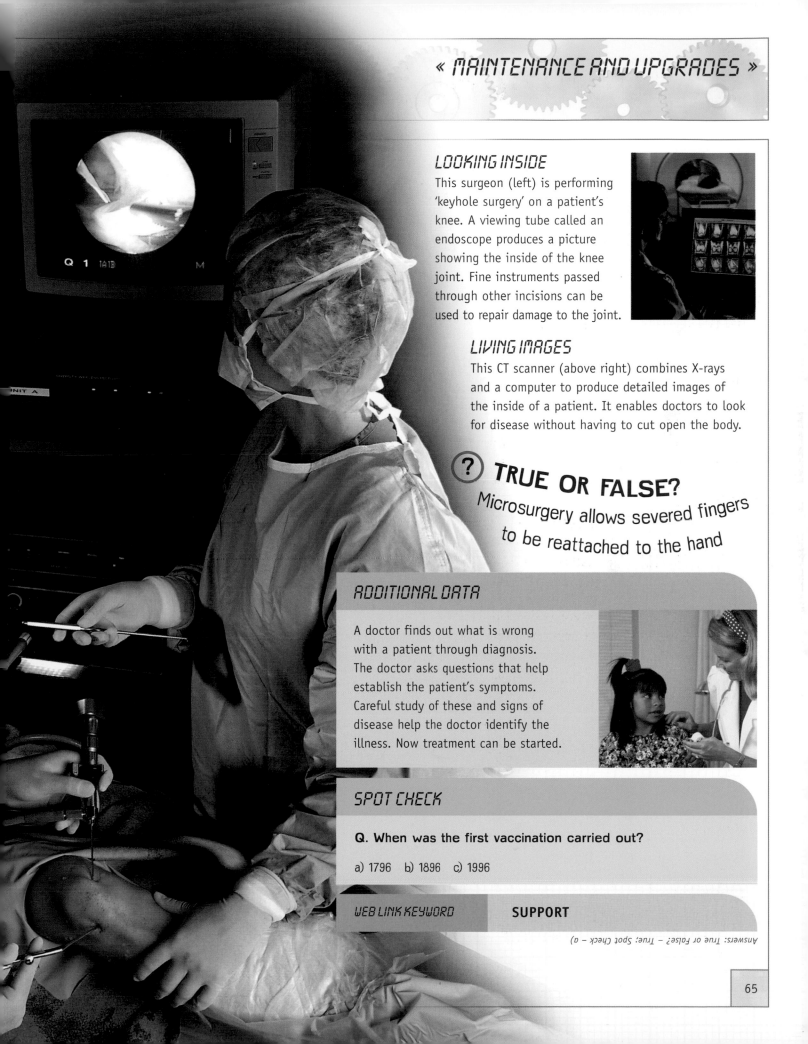

LOOKING INSIDE

This surgeon (left) is performing 'keyhole surgery' on a patient's knee. A viewing tube called an endoscope produces a picture showing the inside of the knee joint. Fine instruments passed through other incisions can be used to repair damage to the joint.

LIVING IMAGES

This CT scanner (above right) combines X-rays and a computer to produce detailed images of the inside of a patient. It enables doctors to look for disease without having to cut open the body.

(?) TRUE OR FALSE?

Microsurgery allows severed fingers to be reattached to the hand

ADDITIONAL DATA

A doctor finds out what is wrong with a patient through diagnosis. The doctor asks questions that help establish the patient's symptoms. Careful study of these and signs of disease help the doctor identify the illness. Now treatment can be started.

SPOT CHECK

Q. When was the first vaccination carried out?

a) 1796   b) 1896   c) 1996

WEB LINK KEYWORD	**SUPPORT**

Answers: *True or False? – True; Spot Check – a)*

TROUBLESHOOTING TIPS

The best way to keep the human machine working smoothly and in tip top condition is to take good care of it. Regular exercise – preferably every day – is important for fitness. It also helps to keep the body's weight at the right level, in combination with eating a balanced diet.

IMPROVED SPECIFICATION

All parts of the body benefit if you keep fit. The brain will work faster and allow you to think more clearly. The heart and lungs will run more efficiently. Bones will be stronger, while muscles will have more pulling power and tire less easily.

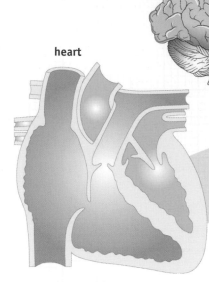

fitness benefits

brain

think quicker, act faster

heart

pump more efficiently

bones

less likely to break

DESIGN FEATURES

- All body organs benefit from high level of fitness
- Exercise improves body machine's stamina, strength and flexibility
- Body machine runs best on fresh, non-processed foods
- Switches to fat mode if overfed and under-exercised

EXERCISE

To stay fit, you need to exercise daily. Regular walking or running increases your stamina – how efficiently your heart, lungs and muscles work. Other activities, such as cycling increase muscle strength. Dance and yoga are good for keeping the body flexible. And swimming increases all three – stamina, strength and flexibility.

? TRUE OR FALSE? Milk contains calcium needed for bone and tooth growth

lungs

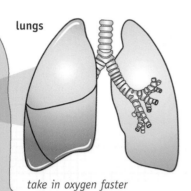

take in oxygen faster

BALANCED DIET

A balanced diet is one that contains a wide range of different fresh foods. The food pyramid provides a guide. The size of each segment shows how much of each type of food the body needs.

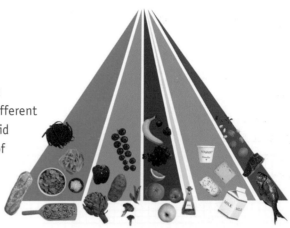

grains　vegetables　fruit　oils and fat　milk　meat, fish and beans

muscles

stronger and tougher

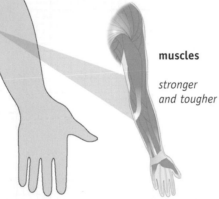

ADDITIONAL DATA

A diet of junk food, combined with a lack of exercise, can lead to serious problems such as obesity, heart disease and diabetes. Junk foods are usually rich in fat, sugar and salt, but lack vitamins and fibre.

RIVAL PRODUCTS

Clay is an important part of the tapir's diet. It is believed that clay particles in the stomach remove poisons found in the plants this animal eats. On chilly mornings, bumblebees need to warm up by 'shivering' before they are able to take off and fly.

SPOT CHECK

Q. Which food is rich in protein, the nutrient needed for body growth and repair?

a) Tomatoes　b) Tuna　c) Pasta

WEB LINK KEYWORD　　　**TROUBLESHOOTING**

Answers: True or False? – True; Spot Check – b)

MECHANICAL FAILURE

Despite having built-in defences and technical support, the body, like any machine, is at risk of mechanical breakdown. General wear and tear or lack of care can result in serious life-threatening problems. These include heart attacks, strokes and some cancers.

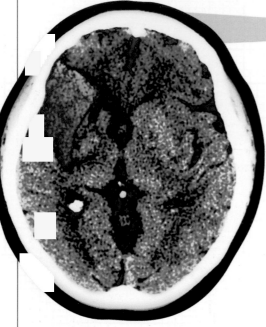

STROKE

When the blood supply to part of the brain is cut off, the result is a stroke, as shown by this red patch on a CT scan of the brain (green). A stroke may be caused by arteries that become blocked or burst. Without oxygen the affected area of the brain stops working properly.

RIVAL PRODUCTS

We are not alone when it comes to mechanical failure. Other animals have heart problems, strokes and cancers, and are treated by veterinary surgeons. Even plants don't escape major breakdowns. A disease called bleeding canker can destroy the bark of trees such as this horse chestnut.

coronary
artery branch

plaque blockage

HEART DISEASE

The coronary artery supplies the beating heart muscle with blood. If there is a build-up of fatty plaque, this can halt the blood supply. In turn, this can lead to a heart attack and stop the heart beating.

(?) TRUE OR FALSE?

Mechanical failure is more likely to happen in older people

CANCERS

This cancer cell (pink) is out of control. Cancer cells are abnormal body cells. They divide uncontrollably to form tumours (lumps) that spread into and stop parts of the body, such as the lungs, working properly. Fortunately, defence cells (blue) usually kill cancer cells before they can multiply and cause harm.

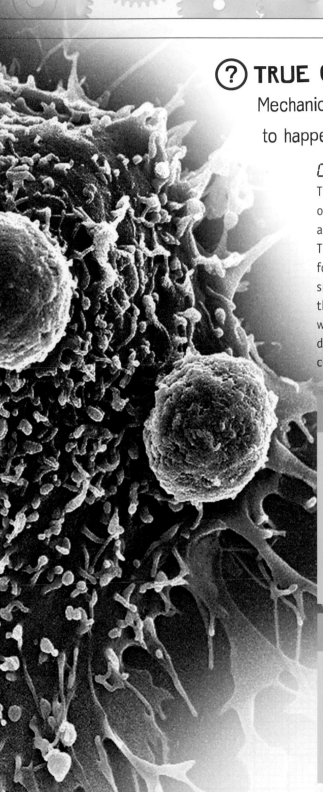

DESIGN FEATURES

- Abnormal cell division can cause cancers
- Blocked or broken blood vessels can upset brain activity
- Blocked blood vessels can stop the heart working properly
- Lifestyle factors such as diet and exercise can increase the risk of mechanical failure

ADDITIONAL DATA

To prevent a heart attack, or to help after one, a medical procedure called angioplasty opens up a blockage in one of the heart's coronary arteries. A small balloon is inflated to widen the blood vessel. A device called a stent is then left behind to keep the vessel open.

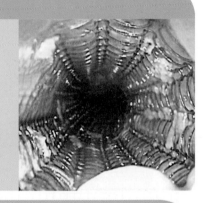

SPOT CHECK

Q. What is the best way to avoid mechanical failure?

a) Eating junk foods
b) Exercising every day
c) Watching TV

WEB LINK KEYWORD   **FAILURE**

Answers: True or False? – True; Spot check – b)

Modern medicine is able to supply the human machine with an increasing range of spare parts to replace components that have been damaged, worn out or lost. These include artificial arms with motorised fingers, replacement joints or new lenses for the eyes. In addition, transplantation means that major organs, such as the heart or kidneys, can be transferred, during an operation, from one human machine to another.

ORGAN TRANSPLANTS

Kidney transplants involve taking a healthy kidney from a suitable donor (giver) – either living or recently deceased – and putting it inside the body of a person with damaged kidneys. Here, the surgeon is attaching the replacement kidney, and connecting it to the blood supply.

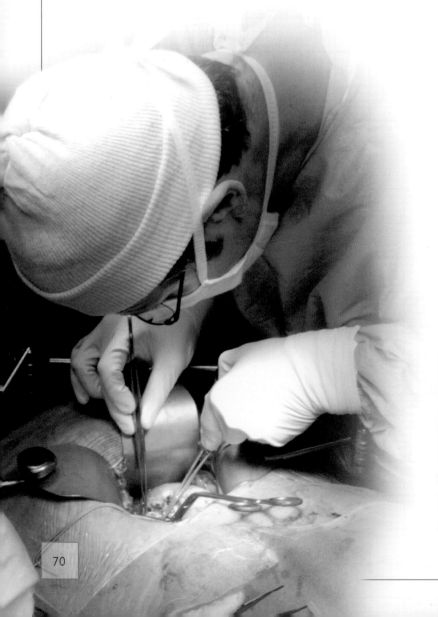

DESIGN FEATURES

- Transplants can replace a damaged heart, kidney, liver, or lung
- Custom-built spare parts made from high-grade metals and plastics
- Potential to grow replacement parts
- Possibility of future upgrades to improve body machine performance

RIVAL PRODUCTS

If humans lose all or part of a limb we would not expect it to grow back. But this process, called regeneration, does happen in 'simple' animals such as starfish. When tree branches are cut back – a process called pollarding – new shoots grow from around the cut area.

spare parts

cochlear implant turns sounds into electrical impulses for deaf people

artificial pacemaker controls heart rate when the natural pacemaker fails

artificial hip joint at top of femur replaces old, diseased joint

lightweight artificial leg with knee and ankle joints replaces amputated limb

Contact lens brings objects into focus

(?) TRUE OR FALSE?

It's possible to transplant a brain from one person to another

SPARE PARTS

The artificial limb is fitted to the stump left after amputation. The other examples require surgery to position them. Contact lenses aren't strictly spare parts, but they improve vision for people who are short-sighted or long-sighted.

GROWING ORGANS

One day it may be routine to grow new, replacement body organs in the laboratory. A start has been made already. By taking bladder cells from a patient, it has been possible to 'grow' a new bladder to replace the patient's defective one.

SPOT CHECK

Q. What is the medical name for a replacement body part?

a) Prognosis b) Prosthesis c) Proboscis

| WEB LINK KEYWORD | SPARE PARTS |

Answers: True or False? – False; Spot Check – b)

WEB LINKS

Look at the bottom of each right hand page in the book and you will find a WEB LINK. For each WEB LINK we have recommended websites that provide additional fascinating information about the human machine in the form of animations, quizzes, and articles. Please note that the content of a website may change at any time, and that neither the publisher nor the author is responsible for any content of the recommended websites.

BIOMECHANICS

www.bbc.co.uk/science/humanbody/body/
interactives/3djigsaw_02/index.shtml?skeleton

http://insideout.rigb.org/ri/anatomy/
casing_the_joint/joints_explorer.html

CELLS

www.icnet.uk/kids/cellsrus/cellsrus.html

www.cellsalive.com/

CIRCULATION

http://www.blood.co.uk/pages/bbits.htm

http://health.howstuffworks.com/adam-200081.htm

COMMUNICATION

www.phon.ox.ac.uk/~jcoleman/phonation.htm

www.pbs.org/wnet/soundandfury/culture/
sign_flash5.html

COMPUTER

http://faculty.washington.edu/chudler/neurok.html

http://health.howstuffworks.com/adam-200008.htm

EMERGENCY

http://health.howstuffworks.com/adam-200012.htm

http://people.howstuffworks.com/fear.htm

FAILURE

http://media.med.cornell.edu/swf/bal_ang.html

http://www.mercymed.com/vascular/discoveries/
images/balloon_stent/balloon_stent.mov

FUEL

www.medicalanimations.com/video.php?num=35&type=mov

http://health.howstuffworks.com/adam-200142.htm

HEAT

http://health.howstuffworks.com/adam-200101.htm

http://www.abpischools.org.uk/resources/skin/skin3.asp

HORMONE

http://health.howstuffworks.com/adam-200091.htm

www.abpischools.org.uk/resources/hormones/index.asp

INSTRUCTIONS

http://gslc.genetics.utah.edu/units/basics/tour/

http://ology.amnh.org/genetics/youYou/youyou.html

LIFESPAN

http://kidshealth.org/kid/grow/body_stuff/puberty.html

www.omsi.edu/visit/life/aging/intro.cfm

MEMORY

www.bbc.co.uk/science/humanbody/mind/surveys/memory

http://faculty.washington.edu/chudler/java/facemem.html

PROTECT

http://health.howstuffworks.com/adam-200096.htm

http://medmyst.rice.edu/html/mission1.html

REPLACEMENT

http://health.howstuffworks.com/adam-200129.htm

http://health.howstuffworks.com/adam-200048.htm

SENSORS

http://health.howstuffworks.com/adam-200010.htm

http://health.howstuffworks.com/adam-200015.htm

http://health.howstuffworks.com/adam-200014.htm

SKIN

http://health.howstuffworks.com/adam-200098.htm

http://magma.nationalgeographic.com/ngexplorer/
0206/quickflicks/

SLEEP

http://science.howstuffworks.com/dream.htm

http://www.brainpop.com/health/nervoussystem/sleep/

SPARE PARTS

www.kidneypatientguide.org.uk/site/TRAanim.php

www.pbs.org/wgbh/nova/eheart/manmade.html

SPECIFICATION

http://kidshealth.org/PageManager.jsp?lic=1&article_set=
29673&ps=110

www.medtropolis.com/VBody.asp

SUPPORT

www.edheads.org/activities/knee/

www.pbs.org/wgbh/aso/tryit/doctor/

SURVIVE

http://www.kativik.net/ulluriaq/Nunavik/inuitlife/
index.html

www.howstuffworks.com/space-suit.htm

TESTS

www.michaelbach.de/ot/

http://lite.bu.edu/vision/applets/lite/lite/lite.html

TROUBLESHOOTING

http://www.coolfoodplanet.org/gb/kidz/

www.lifebytes.gov.uk/eating/eat_menu.html

VENTILATION

http://health.howstuffworks.com/adam-200020.htm

www.bmu.unimelb.edu.au/examples/gasxlung/

VISION

http://health.howstuffworks.com/adam-200013.htm

http://insideout.rigb.org/ri/anatomy/tissue_issues/
eye_eye.html

WASTE

http://www.kidshealth.org/kid/body/kidneys_SW.html

http://health.howstuffworks.com/adam-200032.htm

WIRING

http://health.howstuffworks.com/adam-200011.htm

http://getyourwebsitehere.com/jswb/rttest01.html

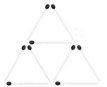

Here's the answer to the brainteaser on page 37.

GLOSSARY

ADOLESCENCE
The period during the teen years when, through a series of physical and mental changes, a child develops into an adult.

ANTIBODY
A chemical released by white blood cells of the immune system that targets a specific disease-causing germ and marks it for destruction.

ARTERY
A thick-walled blood vessel that carries blood away from the heart towards organs and tissues.

ARTHROPOD
One of a very large group of animals without backbones that have a hard outer skeleton and jointed limbs and which include insects, spiders, and crustaceans.

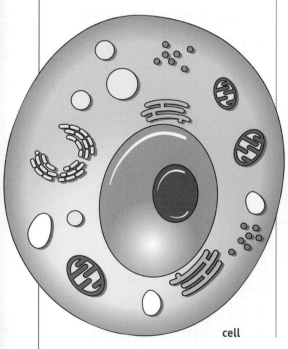

cell

ATRIUM (plural: atria)
One of the two – left and right – upper chambers of the heart.

BACTERIUM (plural: bacteria)
A single-celled organism that belongs to the most abundant group of living things on Earth, some of which cause disease in humans.

BILLION
A number equivalent to one thousand million (1,000,000,000).

CAPILLARY
A microscopic blood vessel that supplies food and oxygen to individual cells in the tissues and links the smallest arteries to the smallest veins.

CARBON DIOXIDE
A gas that is the poisonous waste product of energy release by the cells. It is breathed out into the air from the lungs.

CENTRAL NERVOUS SYSTEM (CNS)
The controlling and co-ordinating section of the nervous system which consists of the brain and spinal cord. It is connected to the rest of the body by nerves.

CEREBRUM
The largest part of the brain, divided into left and right hemispheres, which control opposite sides of the body. The cerebrum is responsible for thought, emotions, sensing, and movement.

DERMIS

The thicker, inner layer of the skin found beneath the protective epidermis. It contains blood vessels, sweat glands, and sensors.

DNA (Deoxyribonucleic acid)

One of a set of large molecules found in the nucleus of every cell. DNA contains the coded instructions to build and operate that cell.

EEG (Electroencephalogram)

A recording of electrical activity in the brain (brainwaves) made by a machine called an electroencephalograph.

ENDOCRINE SYSTEM

A collection of assorted glands, including the pituitary gland, that release chemical messengers called hormones into the bloodstream.

ENZYME

A chemical that greatly speeds up the rate of chemical reactions, including those that break down food during digestion.

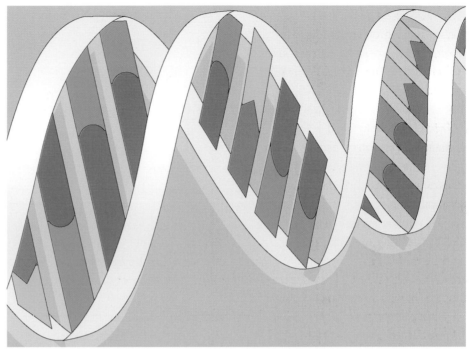

DNA

EPIDERMIS

The thinner, upper layer of the skin above the dermis. The cells of the epidermis are constantly worn away and replaced.

ER (Endoplasmic reticulum)

A network of folded membranes inside a cell that makes, stores and transports substances.

FETUS (FOETUS)

The name given to an unborn child inside its mother's uterus from the ninth week after fertilization.

GENE

One of around 25,000 instructions for making and running a human body stored in the DNA molecules inside cells.

GOLGI BODY

A series of flattened membrane 'bags' found inside cells that package and transport newly-made substances.

GLUCOSE

A sugar obtained from food during digestion that circulates in the blood and provides the body's main source of energy.

HYPOTHALAMUS

A part of the brain that regulates many body activities and links the nervous and endocrine systems.

IMMUNE SYSTEM

The body's defence system which consists mainly of various types of white blood cells that protect against infection by pathogens.

GLOSSARY

INFRARED RADIATION

Rays produced by a hot object such as the Sun that makes us feel warm.

JOINT

The part of the skeleton where two or more bones meet and which enables movement to occur.

LARYNX

Also called the voice box, the part of the respiratory system that contains vocal cords and produces sounds.

LIVER

The body's largest internal organ which performs over 500 functions to control the chemical content of the blood.

MITOCHONDRION

(plural: mitochondria)
One of several spherical or sausage-shaped organelles found inside cells that release the energy needed to power cell activities.

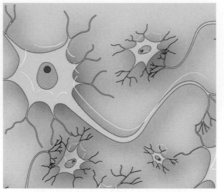

neurons

MOLECULE

A chemical unit made up of two or more linked tiny particles called atoms.

MUSCLE

A body organ or tissue that is capable of contracting (getting shorter) in order to produce movement.

NANOTECHNOLOGY

The branch of technology that involves the construction of structures at the microscopic level using atoms and molecules.

NEURON

One of the billions of interconnected nerve cells that make up the nervous system and can carry high-speed electrical signals called impulses.

NREM (non-rapid eye movement) SLEEP

The stages of deep sleep that recur during the night – between phases of REM sleep – and during which body activities fall to a minimum.

NUCLEUS

The control centre of cell which contains DNA.

NUTRIENT

A substance that your body needs to work properly and keep you alive. Nutrients are found in food and drink.

ORGANELLE

A microscopic structure inside a cell, such as ER or a mitochondrion, that has a specific job to do.

ORGAN

A key part of the body, such as the kidney or brain, that is made up of two or more types of tissue and has one or more specific roles.

OXYGEN

A gas found in the air that is breathed in and used by cells to release energy from glucose.

PATHOGEN

A microscopic organism such as certain types of bacteria, viruses, and protists that cause disease in humans.

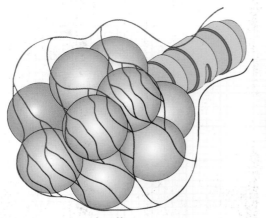

alveoli

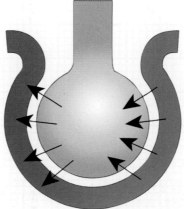

gas exchange

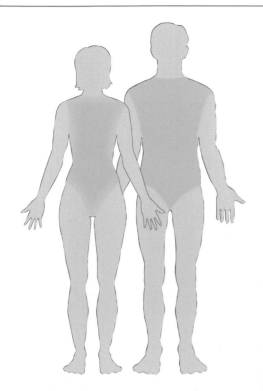

PLASMA
The liquid part of blood that is mainly water. Plasma contains many dissolved substances.

PROTIST
A member of a group of single-celled organisms – larger and more complex than bacteria – some of which cause disease in humans.

REFLEX
An automatic, split-second and unchanging response by the body that often protects it from danger.

REM (rapid eye movement) SLEEP
The stage of lighter sleep that occurs during the night – between phases of NREM (non-rapid eye movement) sleep – when the brain is active, the body apart from the eyes is paralysed, and dreaming takes place.

SKELETAL MUSCLE
The type of muscle that is attached to the skeleton and shapes and moves the body.

TISSUE
A collection of one type, or similar types, of cell that work together to perform a particular function. Different tissues join together to form an organ.

TRILLION
A number equivalent to one million million (1,000,000,000,000).

TRUNK
The central part of the body, consisting of the chest and abdomen, to which the head and limbs are attached. It is also known as the torso.

ULTRASOUND
High-frequency sound waves that are used to produce images inside the body, including those of a developing fetus.

VEIN
A blood vessel that carries blood away from tissues and organs back towards the heart.

VENTRICLE
One of the two – left and right – lower chambers of the heart.

VIRUS
One of a group of very small, non-living chemical packages that cause diseases such as colds, flu and measles. Viruses infect and destroy body cells in order to reproduce.

INDEX

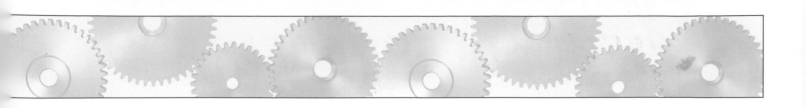

J
joints 24, 25, 65, 76

K
keyhole surgery 65
kidneys 54–55, 70

L
larynx 49, 76
learning 39
lens 44, 45
limbic system 38, 39
limbs 12
lips 49
liver 50, 76
lungs 28, 32–33, 49, 66, 67

M
mammals 13
melanin 18
memory 38–39, 40
metabolism 52
mitochondria 16, 17, 76
molecules 34, 76
moths 53
movement 24, 36
muscles 9, 24–25, 29, 48, 50, 62,
  66, 76

N
nephrons 54
nerves 9, 26, 43
nervous system 9, 26–27, 52
neurons 17, 26, 27, 36, 37, 76
nucleus 16, 20, 76
nutrients 34, 76

O
oesophagus 35
olfactory nerve 43
optic nerve 44, 45
optical illusions 46–47
organelles 16, 76
organs 9, 12, 16, 20, 70, 76

ovaries 53
oxygen 20, 28, 29, 32, 33, 56, 57,
  67, 68, 76

P
pacemaker 71
pathogens 60, 61, 64, 76
personality 36
phobias 39
pituitary gland 52, 53
plaque 68
plasma 29, 77
pregnancy 20–21
protists 61, 77
puberty 53
pulse 29
pupil 44, 45, 63

R
rapid eye movement (REM) 40, 41
reaction times 27
reflexes 62–63, 77
reflexology 64
reproduction 12, 20–21, 52, 53
retina 44
ribs 32

S
saliva 34, 61
scabs 60
sensors 19, 42–43, 44
sex hormones 53
sign language 43
skeleton 9, 24–25
skin 15, 18–19, 50, 51, 60, 63
skull 37, 44
sleep 40–41
smell 38, 42, 43
sounds 43, 49
spare parts 70–71
speech 36, 48, 49
sperm 20
spiders 39
spinal cord 9, 27, 36, 38, 62

stamina 66
starch 34
stomach 34, 35
stress 15, 53
strokes 68
surgery 64–65
swallowing 35
sweat 50, 54, 63
sweat glands 50, 51

T
taste 42, 43
taste buds 42, 43
teeth 34, 49
testes 53
thalamus 38
thinking 26, 36, 38, 66
thorax 12
throat 32
tissues 16, 65, 77
tongue 43, 49
touch 36, 43
trachea (windpipe) 32, 49
trees 35
tumours 69

U
umbilical cord 20
urine 54, 55
uterus (womb) 20
UV (ultraviolet) radiation 18, 19

V
vaccines 64
veins 28, 77
ventricles 28, 77
viruses 60, 61, 77
vision 36, 43, 44–45
vocal cords 49

W
waste disposal 28, 54–55
white blood cells 29, 60
wounds 60

The publishers would like to thank the following for permission to use their material.
Every care has been taken to trace copyright holders. However, if there have been unintentional omissions
or failure to trace copyright holders, we apologise, and will, if informed, endeavour to make
corrections in any future edition.

KEY
t = top; c = centre; b = bottom; r = right; l = left

Peter Homlboe
8–9; 15c; 17l, 18bl; 19tr; 22tc; 22–23; 23tr; 22cr; 24–25; 25tr, 27bl; 29cl; 30–31; 33l; 34l; 36–37; 37cr; 38r; 39bl; 40–41; 42–43;
43bl; 44br; 45tr; 46–47 (illustrations); 48cr; 50–51; 51tr; 52c (illustration); 54cl (illustration); 54–55; 60cl; 62c; 64bl; 75tr; 77br

Getty Images
4–5 (Dr. David Phillips); 14tcl (Georges Gobet/AFP); 18–19 (Mike Powell); 56–57
(James Balog); 57cr (Bob Eisdale); 62–63 (Tom Hussey)

Oxford University Press
1–2; 10–11; 12–13; 13cr; 14c; 14b–15b; 15tc; 19cr; 21; 22tl; 25cr, 27; 29bl; 29cr; 32bl; 32r; 34b; 35br; 38l; 39r; 40br; 42l; 45cr;
48l; 48bl; 50ct; 52–53; 53r; 54cl; 57tl; 57cr; 58–59; 61tc; 62bl; 64–65; 65tr; 65br; 66bl; 67bl; 67cr; 70cr; 74tr; 76tc

Science Photo Library
16b (K H Kjeldsen); 17r (Alfred Pasieka), 20cl (Francis Leroy/Biocosmos); 20c (Dr. G. Moscoso); 20cr (Neil Bromhall); 26bl (Laguna
Design); 29cl (Philippe Plailly/Eurelios); 41bc (Will and Deni McIntyre); 49r (Blair Seitz); 55r (AJ Photo/Hop Americain); 60–61
(Eye of Science); 61cr (James Cavallini) 61cb (Eye of Science); 68tl (Zephyr); 68bl (Mauro Fermariello); 68br (Georgette Douwma);
68–69 (Steve Gschmiessner); 70bl (AJ Photo)

With additional thanks to Alamy (metal cog device), Samir - the scope (69l), USDA Center for Nutrition Policy and Promotion
(67tr), Ventracor Limited for image of VentrAssist™ (29cr)

Models: Matilda Ashford, Tom Ashford, Manny Campion-Dye, Ruben Cleghorn, Oli Jones, Polly Rawlings, Madeline Rolt

Illustrations by Dee McLean/Linden Artists